30 Dakota Prairie

Bread Recipes

and the Art and Science Behind Making Them

Loretta Sorensen

 prairie hearth
publishing, llc

30 DAKOTA PRAIRIE BREAD RECIPES
and the Art and Science Behind Making Them

ISBN: 978-0-578-39283-7
© Loretta Sorensen: Prairie Hearth Publishing LLC

Published by Prairie Hearth Publishing, LLC
2310 Willowdale Rd
Yankton, South Dakota 57078

First printing March 2022

PREFACE

I am so delighted to be able to offer this recipe collection to you! If you've been struggling to learn how to bake bread, I certainly identify!

When I bought a new bread machine in December 2017, I had high hopes of finally turning out those delicious loaves I watched my mother bake all through my childhood.

Still, all I seemed to make were brick-like loaves that no one in my house (or any other house!) wanted to eat.

It looked like not even a bread machine could help. But I couldn't bear to have another kitchen appliance gathering cobwebs on a cupboard shelf.

That's when the magic started! I spent several weeks experimenting with bread recipes and recipe methods. What I learned – the secret to baking beautiful bread in your bread machine EVERY time – is changing one little step in the baking process, to make all the difference – and picture-perfect loaves! All I have learned and now use to bake bread is contained in this book. And the best news, I believe, is that you can take this method and bake all these recipes as well as your own amazing and delicious breads – and they'll be perfect every time!

Are you ready to make loaves that are almost too pretty to eat? Me too! Let's get baking!

*"I would say to housewives,
be not daunted by one failure, nor by twenty.
Resolve that you will have good bread,
and never cease striving after this result
till you have effected it."*
**"Housekeeping in Old Virginia,"
Marion Cabell Tyree (1878)**

CONTENTS

RECIPES

CONTENTS

BEFORE YOU BAKE

HOME-MADE BREAD CHEAT SHEET

If you're fairly experienced with baking bread, here's a quick cheat sheet to get you started on the method that has brought me so much success.

Before you dive into your new bread baking adventure (you're going to love it!), there are some important things to keep in mind:

NOTE: All temperatures referred to in this book are Farenheit.

1. Start with flour and yeast that is no more than 12 months old. That's especially true of yeast. The fresher the ingredients the better your bread will taste.

2. Use proper tools (measuring cups and spoons, mixing bowls, etc.), including bread pans that measure no more than 9x5. Ideal size is 8.5 x 4.5. Using larger pans means bread dough will spread out rather than rise.

3. If you're using glass or thin metal pans, consider placing parchment paper on the bottom of the pan to ensure you can remove the bread once it's baked.

4. I recommend using 8.5 x 4.5 aluminized steel pans (they're

well worth the investment). Whichever pan you use, coat the bottom and sides well with something such as non-stick spray before placing dough in it.

5. Activated yeast likes to be warm (me too!). Warm the liquid your recipe calls for to between 105 and 110 degrees Fahrenheit. Cooler temps keep yeast from activating, hotter temps kill yeast.

6. If it's winter and your house is pretty cool, warm the measuring cup/bowl you use to mix your yeast; warm the bread machine canister and the pan you use to bake bread in the oven (if you're not baking it in the machine). Warming these utensils helps keep the yeast and dough at an appropriate and consistent temperature.

7. Your yeast needs something to eat while it's working on the bread dough! Use your preferred sweetener - sugar, honey, maple syrup, etc. - but don't skip this step.

8. When all your ingredients are ready to go into the bread machine canister, add the yeast mixture first, then gently add the flour mixture, and place the oil/butter, ingredients like molasses, etc. on top.

10. If you can program your bread machine, set it to go through these cycles: mix/knead 15 minutes; rest 20 minutes; mix/knead 10 minutes. These are the cycles you will use for most of the recipes in this book. If your machine doesn't have programming capabilities, simply use a timer to manually start and stop the machine.

11. After about five minutes of the first cycle, check your dough. If it's sticky enough that it sticks to your finger, add flour 2 tablespoons to 1/4 cup at a time. You want a moist dough, but it shouldn't stick to your hand.

12. After the second kneading cycle is complete, you can either finish the bread in the machine (don't do anything, the machine will work through the steps), or place your dough in a bread pan.

13. Your dough's first rise takes place in the bread machine. Since you warmed that canister before using it, your dough will be comfy (and rise nicely!). When it comes out of the bread machine – after the second kneading – make sure you place it in a warmed bread pan and set it in a warm spot (between 80 and 100 degrees is ideal, but at least 70/75) for the final rise.

13. If you're baking your bread in your oven rather than the bread machine, cover your dough during the final rise to keep it from drying out. Moisture enhances yeast action.

14. Once your dough has risen even with or slighly above your bread pan, it's ready to bake. Preheat your oven (typically to 350) and handle the bread pan carefully as you place it in the pre-heated oven. Baking times are generally 30-40 minutes.

15. Use a cooling rack to cool your bread once it's baked. If you don't, you'll have

a loaf with a soggy bottom!

16. Don't place your bread in any kind of storage (plastic bag, bread keeper, etc.) until it's thoroughly cooled. If necessary, you can place a kitchen towel over it and allow it to cool overnight.

17. Once it's thoroughly cooled, store your bread in the refrigerator either in a securely closed plastic bag or a bread storage utensil like Prepworks by Progressive Bread Prokeeper (my favorite). I don't recommend using a bread box because, especially in summer, home-made bread will quickly spoil and mold in this warm, dark environment.

18. You don't need a high end bread machine to produce awesome bread! An inexpensive machine ($35-$50) can pay for itself quickly no matter what type of bread you're making!

19. GET STARTED BAKING! Find my recipes starting on page 41.

NOTE: All temperatures referred to in the book are Fahrenheit.

BEFORE YOU BAKE

WHY USE A BREAD MACHINE?

If you've struggled to make bread with or without a bread machine, then we have traveled the same road!

Occasionally i could produce a wonderfully light loaf of bread using traditional mix, knead, raise, and bake methods. But not very often. And the time and effort involved in baking bread – without using a bread machine – is substantial.

I purchased my machine because i wanted the healthiest possible diet for me and my family. Home-made bread is fresh, has no preservatives, and can be tailored to our needs and tastes.

I'll never forget the day i realized that bread machines – they all have very much the same basic principles – provided two things that more traditional bread making methods cannot:

1. They mix and knead dough longer and more thoroughly than i ever could.

2. They maintain an even and proper temperature that supports yeast activity.

3. I can put all my ingredients in the bread machine canister and walk away for 35 minutes!

These things make bread baking so easy! Once you learn the simple steps to getting the most out of your bread machine, you'll find it is so easy!

If you're considering the purchase of a bread machine, you don't need anything fancy. The bread-making principles i use and have outlined in this book require only one thing: the machine can mix/knead the dough. It's easy to use a timer

to start/stop any bread machine to achieve the cycle sequence i've found to be so effective. You can check the condition of the dough at any time during these cycles, and doing it manually opens the door to a wide, wide range of bread recipes.

If you're using an aging bread machine, all it really needs to do to produce desirable loaves of bread is mix and knead the dough. Once that's done, you can place the dough in a regular bread pan, complete the final rise, and bake it in your oven.

You can use a mixer with a dough hook to do these things, too. One advantage of the machine is that it keeps the dough warm and maintains a consistent temperature until the dough is ready for the final rise. If you opt to use a mixer, take care to keep your dough as consistently warm as possible and don't shortcut the length of mix/knead cycles.

I started out with a hamilton beach homebaker model that cost about $50. Once i learned how to successfully bake my own bread, i have not purchased any kind of bread.

I promise, if you follow the instructions in this book, in regard to preparing your equipment, babying your yeast, and completing the final rise (if you bake the bread in the oven), you are likely to shun store-bought bread for the rest of your life!

BEFORE YOU BAKE

BREAD BAKING TOOLS

The only major tools I don't recommend you do without:
- bread machine
- digital thermometer (you can find them for $5 or less)
- appropriate bread pan – no larger than 9x5 and preferably metal (aluminized is my favorite type)

For some of the tools I've listed here, you can "make do" with a substitute.

Additional toolse:
1. 4-cup measuring cup to mix and start yeast
2. Digital thermometer to test temperature range of liquid
3. Large mixing bowl to measure all dry ingredients
4. Fork to blend dry ingredients.
5. Measuring cups (to match all the measurements called for in your recipe)
6. Measuring spoons
7. A couple small mixing spoons
8. At least one spatula to help thoroughly clear measuring cups of their contents

9. Appropriately sized bread pans
10. Aerosol non-stick spray or pan lubricant of your choice
11. Small cloth/kitchen towel to cover the bread dough for the final rise (unless you finish it in the bread machine)
12. Potholders/oven mitts to remove the baked bread from the oven
13. Cooling rack
14. Storage container for the cooled bread
15. Sharp knife to cut the bread

BAKE

BREAD PAN BASICS

Believe it or not, using the wrong kind of pan (too big, glass, too narrow) can derail your bread baking efforts.

When I started baking bread (or at least attempted to), I used loaf pans I had on hand. It made sense to do so, and I had no reason to believe the pans I had on hand weren't suited to the job. That helps me understand some of my bread-baking flops.

What I have learned over time is that, ideally, bread pans should measure 8.5 inches long and 4.5 inches wide. The maximum recommended size is 9x5.

The reason: when your bread rises, you want it to go up, not out. Loaf pans longer and wider than this will affect the rise of your home baked bread. That wide loaf may not fit into your toaster very well either!

If you use a pan that's too narrow, the top of your loaf will be very wide, and may fall down over the side of the pan. It will be very edible, just not very pretty to look at!

Some of my early bread baking attempts involved baking in glass pans. It was so fun to see the bread raise in the pan, view the browning crust from top to bottom while the bread baked, and keep an eye on the process from start to finish.

However, those wonderful rewards were often crushed when my well-greased glass pan refused to let go of that beautiful loaf! All too often the glass pan managed to cling to a big bite of either the bottom of the loaf, one side, both sides, or all three!

So, I really discourage you from using glass pans, unless you use parchment paper to keep the loaf from stubbornly sticking to the bottom pan. If you do use parchment to line the entire pan, just know that it will affect the shape of your loaf to some degree. It won't lay exactly flat inside your pan. Be sure to securely press the parchment into the corners of your pan to avoid a distorted bottom on the loaf.

You can also cut a piece of parchment that simply fits into the bottom of the pan. A sharp knife may be helpful in prying the baked loaf loose if it sticks to the sides of the pan, but even that can damage the loaf or leave some of it sticking to the side of the pan.

My favorite bread-baking pans are aluminized, 8.5 inches long, 4.5 inches wide. One reason I like them so well is the pan's corrugated feature, which makes it so much easier to slip your baked loaf out of the pan with zero sticking. I still coat them with a liberal amount of non-stick spray.

Another reason I like the aluminized pans is even heating and a lifetime warranty. They do cost more than some other pans but will give the best lifelong service.

If you're making dinner rolls or buns with your dough, pan size isn't as critical. Although your buns will rise higher if they're in a pan that squeezes them together a bit.

BEFORE YOU BAKE

FAST AND EASY

Speed and convenience are two reasons people use bread machines. My method does not include setting the machine up and letting it sit overnight or throughout the day before mixing the dough. I use the machine to get the best activation of the gluten in the flour and to support optimal yeast activity.

Even though my bread making method calls for one extra step not found in standard bread machine recipes, that doesn't mean it requires a great deal of time – or effort!

If I put all my ingredients into my machine and baked the bread in the machine, it would take 3 hours. My method – ending with baking the bread in my oven – takes just a few minutes less than 2 hours.

Here's an approximate time frame for my method of making bread in the bread machine:

1. Collect all your equipment. (5 minutes)

2. Collect all your ingredients. (5 minutes)

3. Put warm water in your bread machine canister and yeast/liquid measuring cup to warm it up. (1 minute)

4. Measure the recipe's liquid ingredients and maple syrup. Check the temperature with a digital thermometer. (1 minute – if your liquid temperature is within the range of 105-110 degrees; 2-3 if you need to warm it up or cool it off)

5. Dissolve the yeast in the liquid, allow it to sit for 3-5 minutes. While it's working, blend all your dry ingredients. (5 minutes)

6. Blend flour, salt, any additional dry ingredients (4 minutes)

7. Empty the warm water out of the bread machine canister. (15 seconds)

8. Pour yeast mixture into bread machine canister. Gently pour flour mixture into the canister. Measure oil (butter, lard, etc.) and add on top of the flour mixture. Close the lid and turn the machine on. (3 minutes)

One additional way to cut down the time involved is to mix the dry ingredients for a recipe and store them until you need them. That would shave off a several minutes.

As you become more familiar with the method and recipe, you could prepare all the ingredients and start your bread machine cycle within 10 minutes or less.

I imagine each bread machine's cycles are similar. I programmed my machine to mix/knead for 15 minutes; rest for 20 minutes; mix/knead for 10 minutes (a total of 45 minutes).

At this point, I have a bread pan sprayed (to prevent sticking) and ready for the dough. It takes about 10 seconds to stretch the dough ball a bit to make it lay across the length of the bread pan. That will give you a nice, even loaf of bread.

Now it should raise in a warm location (80 degrees is ideal but do the best you can) for about 30 minutes (up to 45 minutes if the temperature of the room is 70 degrees or less).

Once the dough reaches two or three inches above the side of the bread pan, it's ready to bake. Heating your oven probably takes around 6 minutes. Don't skip preheating as that rush of heat at the beginning of the bake will cause your yeast to push up into that beautiful dome shape we like to see in a loaf. Baking time will generally be 30 minutes.

So, you can expect your lovely bread loaf to come out of the oven in just about 2 hours after you start the process. If I baked my bread in my machine, I would need 3-hours from start to finish.

The more I bake bread, the more streamlined my process becomes!

BEFORE YOU BAKE

YEAST

What makes it so much more difficult to bake bread versus a cake or cookies? Yeast is a living organism and it's vulnerable to death and inactivity if the environment isn't supportive.

What is yeast? Now, don't cringe, but the definition of yeast is, "a microscopic fungus of single oval cells that reproduce by budding, and are capable of converting sugar into alcohol and carbon dioxide."

That process of converting sugar into alcohol and carbon dioxide (a gas), is what makes the bread rise. The fermentation yeast undergoes (in a warm environment) helps strengthen and develop gluten, which occurs naturally in wheat and some other grains.

Gluten is a protein which is further developed during kneading, giving dough strength and elasticity. The more thorough the kneading, the stronger the gluten, which then traps the carbon dioxide and gives bread dough a "lift."

Yeast is activated by moisture and temperatures that are 95 degrees or more. At a temperature of 115 degrees or more, yeast will die.

Salt and artificial sweeteners kill yeast, as will a lack of sugar it needs to feed on.

These are all the reasons to:

1. Ensure the temperature range of your recipe liquid supports yeast activity, not too cold, not too hot. Ideal: 105-110 degrees Fahrenheit.

2. When activating yeast, use sugar, honey, or maple syrup to "feed" it.

3. Maintain that warm temperature throughout the mixing, kneading and rising process to get the best "rise" in your bread dough.

SO MANY YEAST PRODUCTS!

In years past, I sometimes purchased cake yeast (a wet, compressed yeast product) at my local bakery. It worked fine, but active dry yeast is much more practical, and the only yeast form I use now.

If you're looking to control bread baking costs, I recommend purchasing dry yeast in a 16 ounce or 32-ounce package. Both options are much less expensive than buying the individual packages or even the little jars of yeast commonly found on grocery shelves. There's no need to buy "bread machine yeast."

Whatever type of yeast packaging you purchase, it's wise to refrigerate or freeze the yeast because it will retain quality far longer than it does on the shelf.

If you use one- or two-pound packages of yeast, be sure to use a canister or jar of some kind that tightly seals it to help maintain quality.

YEAST LIFE SPAN

Since it's a living organism, yeast is perishable.

Your best bet is to store yeast in an airtight container in your refrigerator or freezer, protecting it from heat or unwanted moisture.

I have found that active dry yeast maintains its quality for a minimum of 6 months in the refrigerator and up to 12 or 18 months in the freezer.

For optimum bread baking results, baby your yeast (in terms of temperature) all through the baking process. As much as possible, keep your dough in an 80-degree (Fahrenheit) environment. I like to warm my oven and allow the dough to make its final rise there. Just don't get too much heat, or the yeast will die before it can complete its work!

BEFORE YOU BAKE

WHAT ABOUT FLOURS?

It was a great relief to me to find that the baking method I've outlined for you works equally well with either standard white flour or whole grain flours.

Generally, I bake with a mix of white and whole grain flours. Many people don't like the strong taste of red wheat, but white wheat flour, a whole grain, has a much less intense wheat flavor. A white wheat loaf will look nearly identical to a white flour loaf.

No matter which type of flour you select, it must be fresh. White flour on the shelf will keep for 6-10 months. Whole grains must be stored either in the refrigerator or freezer to prevent their oil content from becoming rancid.

I store my flour in airtight, high quality plastic containers (to avoid leaching of toxic elements from the plastic). When you think about it, bread is often a daily staple for many families. It's well worth investing in quality flour containers to ensure we produce the healthiest bread possible.

On average, there are at least four different types of flour in my pantry at any one time. For that reason (and the fact that my memory doesn't always serve me that well!), I label and date my flour. Any kind of label will do, but I highly recommend labeling and dating flours. There's nothing more disappointing than going to the work of baking bread only to find you didn't use the flour you thought you did or that it has an "old" taste to it because it wasn't as fresh as you believed.

White flours, which have the wheat bran removed during processing, keep longer at room temperature than whole

grain products. The oil content of whole grains will take on a rancid taste if it's too old or is subjected to high temperatures very long. Whole grain flour is also more susceptible to bug infestations. My whole grain flours are stored in the freezer or refrigerator unless I expect to use them within a couple of weeks.

WHOLE GRAINS

White wheat has become a popular choice of bread bakers (even commercial ones) in recent years. White wheat is still a whole grain, just a different variety from regular whole wheat.

White wheat loaves look lighter than standard wheat bread. My favorite aspect of white wheat is the sweeter, less intense taste it gives bread and other baked goods.

Both regular wheat and white wheat berries (the name for the harvested wheat grains) can be ground into flour.

Other whole grains can be used in baking bread, however wheat results in the lightest, highest rising loaves. Grains like spelt, millet, barley, etc. can be mixed with wheat – either whole grain or white flour – to bake bread. Mixed grain bread is delicious, and when you use a bread machine to make it, you still get a wonderful high rise.

You'll find a variety of whole grain flours in most grocery stores. You can also search out online sources for different flours.

My favorite whole grain

sources for both flour and whole grain kernels:
To Your Health at
www.healthyflours.com

Sunrise Flour Mill at
www.sunriseflourmill.com

There are many other sources, too.

Breads made with ready-to-use flours will taste wonderful. However, whole grains, ground shortly before using them, gives bread a very fresh taste (provided the grains are fresh). Whole grains can be stored in the freezer for 12 months or more

GRINDING WHOLE GRAINS

Before I ground my first grains, I believed I might need a grain mill in order to get a flour fine enough for baking. I was wrong!

My high-powered blender, a Vitamix (using a dry grinding canister), ground my grains beautifully in just moments. I also use a Kitchen Aid grinder attachment. Neither process is fast, but it's fairly easy to dedicate some time to grinding the grain and storing it in the freezer until I'm ready to use it. Today's blenders have much more power than they used to, so you may want to try grinding a bit of whole grain in your blender before investing in a grain mill or a more expensive blender.

Using a blender to grind your grain will result in having some "grainy" texture to your flour. I enjoy that characteristic

in my breads. If you want finer flour, you could sift it before using it.

If you're using freshly ground flour, make sure you don't skimp on the liquid in your bread recipe because your flour will absorb a bit more liquid than ready-to-use varieties.

My experience with grinding whole grains has been that one cup of wheat berries (or other grains) will result in slightly more than 1 cup of flour. If you grind more flour than you can use in your recipe, simply store it in the refrigerator or freezer until you can use it.

MEASURING FLOUR

When you measure your flour in cups, make sure you don't pack the flour tightly into the measuring utensil, because you'll end up using more flour than your recipe calls for. I recommend using a flour scoop (or a good-sized spoon) to scoop up your flour and place it in the measuring cup. Even then, be careful not to pack flour into the scoop or spoon.

When measuring flour, use a knife (or the edge of your scoop) to level the cup. While your bread machine is working, you can easily look inside it and determine if you need to add a bit more flour. About five minutes into the first mix/knead cycle, check the dough. If it sticks to your hand, it needs more flour. But don't overdo it! Add 2 tablespoons to ¼ cup at a time because dry dough will not rise well.

If you become super serious

about baking, you may consider weighing your flour and using a specific number of ounces of flour rather than measuring it out in cups. I have not had good success with this method. At least not yet!

Keep in mind that your dough should be just a little sticky when you put it in your pan for the final rise. If you can coat your hands with a bit of oil and easily shape your dough to fit into your bread pan, you've used enough flour.

The reason recipes call for volumes such as 3-4 cups of flour is that humid conditions may require adding a bit of additional flour. Cold, dry winter conditions usually mean you can use a little less flour.

Always start with the lesser amount and add enough to get a dough that's moist but doesn't stick to your hand when you touch it.

BEFORE YOU BAKE

TELL ME ABOUT KNEADING

Historians (A Brief History of Bread," History.com) estimate that humans began baking some form of bread "at least 30,000 years ago."

But it wasn't until about 300 B.C. that bread bakers captured yeast – which actually floats through the air, looking for a satisfactory environment where it can grow.

Yeast is the most common bread "leavening," which means it's most often used to produce the soft, fluffy bread that's so irresistible!

The Egyptians are credited with producing the first commercial yeast production around 300 B.C.

Kneading dough dates back nearly as far as those first bread bakers. What bakers discovered decades ago is that kneading affects the two proteins found in wheat flour: gliadin and glutenin. These proteins combine to form gluten, which adds to the fluffiness and rise of bread dough.

It also improves the texture and taste of the bread, as well as creating a "to-die-for" crust.

This is where a bread machine shines. My machine mixes and kneads my dough for 15 minutes in the first kneading cycle. After a 20-minute rest, the machine kneads the dough for another 15 minutes. Even if I was ambitious enough (and strong enough) to knead my dough that long, I couldn't achieve the same results as my bread machine.

All that kneading creates a structure within the dough to trap the gas the yeast gives off and push that dough to lofty (and might I say beautiful!) heights. For me, this means I will never be without a bread machine again.

If you're in the market for a bread machine, no need to purchase the most expensive one. Especially if you plan to bake your bread in the oven. I rarely bake in my bread machine because I prefer the size and shape of a standard loaf – and I can make my bread in two hours that way, versus three hours in my bread machine.

If you have an aging or second-hand bread machine that successfully kneads your dough, no need to look for a newer model. You can produce incredible loaves with very little effort.

BEFORE YOU BAKE

BREAD BAKING COSTS

Basic home made bread costs less than commercial loaves, especially bakery-style loaves.

However, it's relatively easy to spend a significant amount of money on homemade bread if you're not paying attention to the cost of high quality and/or organic flours.

When determining what flours you want to use, balance nutrition and quality against total cost. The quality of homemade bread is higher than a commercial loaf because it can be made with ingredients that contain no preservatives or obscure chemicals.

If you prefer the quality and/or results of using a higher cost flour, consider the option of blending a more expensive product with one you can purchase at a lower price.

For instance, I love using bread flour. However, it is often nearly twice as expensive as all-purpose flour. To find a happy medium, I started mixing bread flour and all-purpose flour half and half. It's all organic, the all-purpose flour cuts the total cost by at least 50%, and I'm still delighted with my bread.

If you're really pinching pennies, there's no reason all-purpose flour – at less than half the cost of bread flour – won't produce a highly satisfactory loaf of bread. In fact, you may find you can use just a bit less all-purpose flour in your recipe. Experiment with it a bit and see what works best. If you want to improve the overall rise of your bread, you can add an egg to enhance the rise.

If like me, you appreciate sprouted grains and flours, there are a couple of ways to incorporate them into your bread baking with busting your budget.

If you're willing to sprout your own grains, you will save the most. This requires careful monitoring of the grain as it's germinating and a process for thoroughly drying it once it is sprouted. It may be possible to sprout just the amount of grain you need for a recipe and immediately use it in your baking. I need to test that out!

If you're less adventurous, you can save money by purchasing whole sprouted grains. There is a difference in cost between sprouted grains and sprouted organic grains. Organic products are generally more pricey. For me, they're well worth it.

It literally takes seconds to grind enough grain to produce flour for baking a loaf of bread. About 30 seconds per half cup is all that's necessary. You need approximately 3.5 cups for a medium loaf of bread, so you'll spend around 5 minutes grinding grain. And you will love the flavor!

If neither sprouting your own grain nor grinding whole grain appeals to you, it's easy to mix the more expensive flour with something less costly and still have a high-quality bread that fits your budget.

You might also consider replacing a higher cost item (i.e., meat) for a meal that consists of whole grain bread and nut butter or eggs, vegetable or bean soup, etc. The money saved by substituting the cheaper, yet highly nutritious bread could be used to help pay for flour.

Overall, you may find that homemade bread provides so many health benefits to you and your family and saves so much in comparison to purchasing bakery-style breads that no flour is off limits in terms of costs.

BEFORE YOU BAKE

IT'S ALL ABOUT RISING!

As soon as your bread machine completes the second kneading cycle, you can place the dough in a warmed, well-coated bread pan for the final rise (or let it bake in your machine).

Be sure your bread pan is coated with either non-stick spray, lots of butter, olive oil, etc. so your bread slips out easily once it's baked. Nothing worse than having a big chunk of your loaf stick in the pan. Tearing out a chunk can also make slices irregular and difficult to toast because they lose their shape.

Parchment paper can work on the bottom of the pan. However, my experience in lining my bread pan with parchment resulted in an odd-shaped bottom on the loaf.

My favorite spot for this final rise is in my oven. Before the bread is ready to rise, I turn my oven on briefly to add a shot of warm air that helps keep the temperature near 80 degrees. You don't want the oven to be too warm, as your pan will absorb that heat and threaten your yeast. Too hot and your yeast

dies before the dough is ready to bake. Don't warm the oven to more than 100 degrees.

You also want to cover the dough with either a paper towel, dish towel or some type of small towel that covers the dough during the final rise. This helps trap heat to support yeast activity and retain moisture in the dough until the bread is ready to bake.

It typically takes 30-40 minutes for this final rise. Once the dough is two or three inches above the side of your bread pan (an oval shape rising up out of the pan), it's ready to bake.

If you raised your dough in the oven, carefully remove it for preheating the oven. Handling it too roughly could cause it to flatten.

Set your pan in a draft-free area while your oven heats. Keep the dough covered until it's ready to go into the oven.

Follow the oven settings in your recipe (typically 350 degrees Farenheit). For the best results, allow the oven to fully heat before placing the bread inside. Generally it takes 30 minutes for the loaf to bake thoroughly.

Once you remove the bread from the oven, immediately remove it from the pan and place it on a cooling rack. Make sure the loaf is completely cool before storing it in any kind of container. It works well to cover the loaf with a dish towel while it completes its final cooling. This helps keep the crust from drying too much. If necessary, you can leave the towel on the loaf overnight.

BEFORE YOU BAKE

FLOUR: STORE BOUGHT OR FRESH GROUND?

Should I start my bread baking with flour from the store shelf or try to grind my own?

Early in my bread-baking efforts I wanted to answer this question. Since every baker has different goals, there's no one "right" answer.

Certainly, if taking time to grind your own grain would stall or even end your bread-baking activities, use the milled flours you are able to purchase. With all our buying options – in-store, online, direct from growers, etc. – it's generally not difficult to obtain quality flour for your bread.

And with online purchase options, there's certainly a wide range of brands and flour types at our fingertips.

Here's a summary of advantages for both purchasing milled flour and making your own!

Purchasing milled flour:

• Big time saver
• Finely milled to give you a fine bread texture
• Ability to purchase in quantities large enough for making multiple loaves
• Consistent quality and texture

Grind your own grain
• Ability to manage freshness by grinding the grain shortly before or right before using it
• Create customized grain blends
• Obtain coarse grind flours
• Verify growing conditions (grow yourself or purchase from known grower)

Of course, there are some disadvantages to grinding your own grains. One main hurdle is purchasing proper grinding equipment. Most modern blenders will grind grain. Depending on the blender's power, the flour may be quite coarse. Grinding the flour twice will usually give you the results you want.

Personally, I love a coarse grind to bake my bread. Some visible pieces of the whole grain and bran show up in your loaf. However, if you have someone with digestive/colon issues, those little bits of grain may cause problems. Sifting is fast and easy and will pull out those coarse grain pieces. You may want to consider grinding them again to maximize use of your whole grains.

While you can create customized grain blends by grinding whole grains, there's no reason not to use milled flours to make grain blends

that help you reach your baking goals.

One of my common grain blends is wheat and rye. We enjoy rye bread on occasion. Since rye has less gluten than wheat, my loaves are most satisfactory if I blend 50% wheat flour with 50% rye flour. (If you use this blend, boost your kneading cycles to 18 minutes each to maximize your gluten activity.)

If you're experimenting with grain blends to find personal taste, nutrition, and texture preferences, using milled flour will be faster and may be less expensive.

Grinding your own grain is much easier than you may have imagined. Using a Vitamix blender (use the dry container), you can grind approximately 4 cups of flour in just 5 minutes or less. This will be a somewhat coarse grind, but easily fine enough for baking bread.

If you prefer to mill your own grain, be prepared to invest in a quality grain mill. Some of the highest rated home mills cost at least $500. You may also want to consider how much storage space you have for a mill before you buy one. They're not huge but will require a significant amount of storage space.

My goal is to invest in a mill so I can produce the fine flours my family prefers. Once I reach that point, I expect to grind enough flour for 2 or 3 months. Stored in the freezer, they will retain their quality for at least 6 months.

It's not necessary to grind your own grain to bake bread, but there's a certain satisfaction that comes with preparing your own bread flour. Once you learn how fast and easy it is, it may be the only type of flour you use.

BEFORE YOU BAKE

EVALUATE YOUR RECIPE

Once you perfect a bread-baking method for traditional yeast bread, it's likely you'll want to expand your bread recipe options.

Online recipe resources can be a great place to find new bread recipes. However, use some caution in recipe selection. Not every online recipe is valid.

Some tips for finding valuable, genuine bread recipes online include:

• Rely on well-known brand name sites, i.e. Mother Earth Living, Grit Magazine, Mother Earth News, Taste of Home, The Pioneer Woman, etc.

• To determine whether or not a bread recipe is truly tried and tested, look for these basic elements in a yeasted recipe: flour, liquid (water, milk, etc.), yeast, sweetener to feed the yeast, salt, oil/butter.

• For sourdough, ½ cup starter plus ¾ cup water and approximately 4 cups of flour is a good balance. Be wary of ingredients with a balance far different from this.

• Additional bread ingredients may include molasses, buttermilk, potatoes, nuts, seeds, etc.

• For bread machines, check your machine manual to verify the largest loaf your machine is able to produce. If your recipe calls for more than 6 cups of flour, you may want to use a stand mixer or food processor as this much flour will produce a sizable volume of dough. Regularly overloading your bread machine (or mixer) will burn out the motor.

• To validate yeast amounts, rely on using as little as 1 teaspoon or up to 2 ¼ teaspoons per 4 cups of flour for bread, up to 4 teaspoons yeast to 4 cups of flour for sweet rolls.

If your recipe calls for any of these methods, you may want to reconsider using it:

• Adding salt to the yeast mixture. This will immediately kill yeast. Salt should always be blended with the flour before it's mixed with the rest of the ingredients.

• Omitting sweetener. Your yeast in a standard loaf must feed on something – syrup, honey, brown sugar, milk, etc. – in order to produce a rise.

• Most bread recipes call for three parts flour to one-part liquid (i.e. three cups of flour for 1 cup of water). Overdoing flour in relation to the liquid will result in a dry, dense, and disappointing loaf.

•Cold temperatures for recipe liquids. Yeast will not begin to grow unless liquid temperature is at least 100 degrees. Ideal temperature range is 105- to 110-degrees.

• Hot temperatures for recipe liquids. Liquid temperatures over 115-degrees will kill the yeast.

• Minimal kneading. In traditional yeast breads, kneading activates gluten in the flour, which greatly contributes to the rise.

• Use of an unusually large or small loaf pan. A too-large pan can cause your bread dough to spread out rather than rising up. If your loaf pan is too small, it flows over the side of the pan.

If you've identified a recipe that seems to be legitimate, don't hesitate to do a test run before you rely on producing a beautiful loaf of bread.

Ideally, check all your bread-making supplies the day before you plan to bake to ensure you're not lacking a key ingredient.

Read ALL the instructions, from the beginning of the recipe to the end. This will make you aware of any out-of-the-ordinary rising/baking times or steps you may not otherwise anticipate.

If you modify any portion of the recipe, make a note of it right in your recipe book or on the recipe copy, ensuring you recall the steps that gave you the bread of your dreams!

It can be helpful to maintain all your favorite bread recipes in one book, folder or file. This saves time and allows you to quickly compare a new recipe to tried and tested ones.

DELICIOUS ROLLS
Mrs. Sam (Ella) Borntreger
Seymour, IA

2 c. scalded milk
½ c. sugar
½ c. brown sugar
1 c. water
1 heaping T. yeast
3 c. flour

10 T. melted butter
4½ tsp. salt
Dash of ginger and
2 eggs, beaten
4-5 c. flour

When milk and water is lukewarm, add sugars and yeast. Add flour and stir until smooth. Let stand 15-20 minutes. Then add 4-5 cups flour. Add butt and salt, stirring after each addition. Let rise twice, then roll out and cut. Add b into a soft dough. Let rise again in pa brown sugar and cinnamon before rolling. about 20-30 minutes, then bake 20 minutes at 350°.

♥ OVERNIGHT ROLLS ♥
Mrs. Mose H. Miller
Augusta, WI

2¼ c. water
1 c. sugar
1 stick butter
2 eggs, beaten

Sauce:
4 c. brown sugar
c. butter
c. cream

1 tsp. vanilla
8 c. flour
2 T. salt
1 T. yeast

2 T. Karo
Nuts, add las

yeast in ½ cup warm water
M. Work out before
Be sure

BEFORE YOU BAKE

5 REASONS BREAD DOESN'T RISE

There are nearly as many bread recipes as cooks out there. If you've found a recipe that works well for you, I applaud you!

It has taken me many years and plenty of flour to find both a recipe and method that work well for me and my family.

If, like me, you've struggled to produce a light, fluffy, tasty loaf of bread, I have good news. This method works! And here is why:

1. The yeast is warm enough to be activated.
2. There's just the right amount of flour.
3. Two 15-minute kneading cycles help develop gluten in the flour.
4. The final rise is completed in a warm environment.
5. I preheat the oven to 350 degrees (Fahrenheit).

These five steps are critical to achieving the high-rise loaf that's almost too pretty to eat! I'm happy to explain each one.

1. Yeast will not activate until it's exposed to a temperature of at least 95 degrees. However, that's the minimum temperature to get minimum yeast activity. To fully activate the amount of yeast your bread recipe calls for, the liquid it's dissolved in should be between 105 degrees and 110 degrees. That is the optimum temperature to stimulate yeast activity. If the liquid is more than 112 degrees, the yeast will die. That temperature is too hot. Use a digital thermometer to verify that your recipe liquid is

in the ideal temperature range and your yeast will bloom! And do activate the yeast in water that contains sweetener of some kind – sugar, honey, maple syrup, etc.

2. As your dough raises, the yeast needs moisture to remain active. If you use too much flour, the yeast doesn't have adequate moisture, which will hinder the rise. The loaf will be flatter, dense and not nearly as tasty.

3. There are bread recipes that don't require kneading. Typically, the rise times for those recipes is three-plus hours. These types of recipes generally produce a low-rising loaf. If you want to produce a high-rise loaf of bread within a two-hour time period, include two 15-minute knead cycles in your dough prep method. This develops the gluten in the flour you use, which goes hand in hand with a high rise.

4. Since the yeast in your bread recipe will be active throughout the dough prep and final rise, it's important to keep the bread dough in an environment that doesn't rob the heat yeast needs to continue working. Most ovens are an ideal place to complete the final rise. If desired, you can warm the oven slightly before placing your bread pan inside it.

5. Once your bread dough has risen to the top of the pan, or an inch or so above it, you can set the dough aside (on top of the oven works well) and preheat the oven to 350 degrees. When we're in a hurry, it's tempting to put the dough in the oven before it reaches 350 degrees. However, doing so may hinder the final rise, as that warm temperature provides the last little push yeast needs to bring the bread dough to its loftiest height.

If you're in the process of finding a traditional bread recipe and method that works for you, these tips can help you achieve the kind of beautiful loaf you might hate to cut into!

BEFORE YOU BAKE

BARTER WITH BREAD

The idea of trading one product for another – bartering – goes clear back to 6000 B.C. when tribes in Mesopotamia traded goods with Phoenicians. The practice was also used in Babylon.

The origin of the word barter goes back to the 15th century, stemming from the French word "barater," which, among other things, meant "haggle."

America's barter system was very popular during the Great Depression of the 1930s, when many people had little money. Bartering was a means of obtaining food and other necessities.

When I was approached about the possibility of trading bread for other products – including naturally raised beef – I could hardly say no!

Since I had already calculated the value of a loaf of homemade white bread – which ranges between $1 and $1.50 – it was fairly easy to strike a deal on a fair trade for one pound of the beef. Two loaves of white bread – 100% organic – for one pound of beef, 100% natural.

It has proven to be a beneficial trade on both sides.

Since that trade has been working so well – and I find it so easy to produce a quality loaf of bread – I've been pondering more options for making a trade.

In rural areas – and perhaps more often now in urban areas, too – farm fresh eggs aren't hard to find. If the eggs are organic and laid by free range hens, the cost of a dozen eggs may well be equal to two loaves of bread. Of course, that depends on the flour and other nutrients used in the bread.

When you're baking 100% whole grain bread, it has a value of at least $6 per loaf. If your recipe includes added nutritional ingredients such as flax, the total cost of a loaf may be somewhat higher.

Once you've determined what you have invested in your bread loaves, compare it with the cost of purchasing the item you will take in trade. Your objective is to complete a trade that's fair for all parties involved.

When I bartered for the beef, we struck a deal that covered a weekly trade for about 12 weeks. You may want to make a one-time trade or set up a once-a-month agreement. The terms of the agreement are totally in your control.

In the case of bartering for homemade bread, be careful not to overestimate your ability to produce enough bread to cover your trade agreement.

You may also want to strike a deal with your bartering party that includes how you will amend the agreement or "catch up" with your trade agreement if for some reason you can't produce the promised loaves.

One added benefit of this kind of agreement is that you will have ample opportunity to polish your bread baking skills and promote your bread quality and availability if you're wanting to make more trades or sell some of your bread.

BEFORE YOU BAKE

RECYCLE BOTCHED BREAD

If you're baking bread on a regular basis, every now and then it will happen: a flop!

While a failed loaf of bread falls far short of an economic catastrophe, it still makes me wince to toss one out. So, I recycle it!

The simplest use for either a failed loaf or stale bread is to dry it and use it for bread crumbs, croutons, stuffing, etc.

Generally, my unsatisfactory loaves just didn't raise well for some reason. The healthy ingredients – organic flours, Himalayan salt, milk, sweetener, etc. – are perfectly fine to use. Just not as a slice of bread!

If you've checked the grocery store recently, you know the cost of bread crumbs is plenty high. This greatly elevates the value of your disappointing loaf since you can make several cups of bread crumbs from an entire loaf.

You might also consider using the loaf as it is – without drying it – as filler for dishes like meat loaf, stuffing, bread pudding, etc. Some macaroni and cheese recipes and other types of casseroles call for bread crumb topping. The dried, grated bread also makes great breading for friend foods such as fish, chicken, etc.

If you can't use an entire loaf at once, simply slice it, place either plastic or parchment paper between each slice, freeze and use as needed. The slices will probably dry to some degree if they're in the freezer very long, but that won't have any adverse effect on your recipes!

To dry the bread, slice it or cut it up into crouton shapes/sizes or just small pieces. The small pieces are easier to work with when you shred it into crumbs.

It can take up to 48 hours to dry the bread. During that time, you can cover it with a light weight towel or paper towel. You can also warm up your oven a bit and set the bread in the oven to speed drying. I don't recommend leaving the oven on very long or using a high oven heat. Just a little warmth to get the drying process started.

If the weather is warm and humid when you're trying to dry the bread, you may want to consider using the oven on low heat to avoid providing a resource for mold to start growing.

Once the bread is thoroughly dried, you can shred it or break it up into the sizes and shapes you desire. Either a food processor or blender can be used to shred the dried bread.

After shredding, you'll want to store it in an airtight container. If you don't want to store the crumbs/croutons at room temperature, you can freeze them. Avoid storing them in the refrigerator as there is a significant risk that it will gather moisture and spoil.

It's advisable to label and date the crumbs/croutons so there's no doubt what you're using and how long you've had it stored.

If you have no household use for dried bread products, you might consider feeding it to birds or chickens.

No matter how you use it, always consider recycling left over or unsatisfactory bread products!

BEFORE YOU BAKE

STORING YOUR BEAUTIFUL LOAVES

My experience with home-made bread is that it keeps in the refrigerator for as long as two weeks (if you don't eat it all first!).

At room temperature, no matter the storage method, home-made bread will quickly mold, especially in summer with warm, moist weather conditions.

Purchasing a special storage item for your bread may seem an unnecessary cost. However, I've found that storing bread in a container such as the Prep Solutions by Progressive Bread ProKeeper, keeps the bread fresher longer. This particular storage item is adjustable to expand or contract according to the loaf size. I have used it for four years with great success.

The ProKeeper also avoids moisture collection along the sides and bottoms on your loaf. You will see that problem in a plastic bag. The moisture can hasten spoilage, too. I've never had any of my bread spoil in the Prokeeper.

You are likely to find that your bread loaves don't fit into a standard one-gallon plastic bag. They're just too big! Two-gallon bags are available at a reasonable cost. I use the bags only for bread that I'm gifting. Otherwise, I use my ProKeeper, stored in the refrigerator.

Know that your bread, if left uncovered either at room temperature or in the refrigerator, will dry quickly. That is especially true once its sliced.

Use a sharp knife to slice your bread. If the loaf is still cooling, cut it carefully to avoid flattening the loaf.

BEFORE YOU BAKE

SOUR-DOUGH STARTER

If you're learning how to develop a sourdough starter, it will take 7 days before the starter is ready to use in a bread recipe for the first time. Here's a summary of the starter process:

Key points:

1. Use stainless steel, wooden, or silicone mixing spoons.
2. Always mix ingredients in either a stainless steel or glass/ceramic bowl.
3. Use standard unbleached flour - it helps keep "feeding" costs low.
4. When you "feed" your starter, mix the flour and water in well. Use filtered water or water that has set overnight to diffuse the chlorine because chlorine may interfere with the yeast activity.
4. Refrigerate the starter removed at each feeding (discard) . It can be used right away or within a few days.
5. Before you use the starter in dough, feed it and allow it to sit at room temperature for 10-12 hours so it's at peak strength.

Day 1: To begin the starter: Mix 1 cup flour and 1/2 cup water in a stainless steel or glass mixing bowl. Use water that is room temperature or between 60 and 90 degrees. Place the mixture in a clean quart jar, glass container, or sourdough crock. Cover the top of your container with either a paper towel, cheese cloth, or (for jars) a screen that fits inside the jar ring - this allows air exchange. Allow the starter mixture to sit at room temperature for 24 hours before feeding it.

Day 2: You may see bubbles, but if not go ahead and feed the starter. It will begin "working." To feed: remove 1/2 cup of the starter and add it to a stainless steel or glass mixing bowl. Discard any remaining starter. Add 1 cup flour and 1/2 cup water. Thoroughly combine the flour/water mixture and allow it to sit at room temperature for 24 hours.

Day 3-5: By now (48 hours after first mixing) you should see bubbles starting to form and it should have a fresh, slightly tangy aroma. For the next four days, you will feed the starter two times per day, with 12 hours between feedings. Before removing any of the starter give it a good stir to release any bubbles that have formed. Remove a heaping ½ cup of the starter and place it in a stainless steel or glass mixing bowl. Discard any remaining starter. Add 1/2 cup flour mixed with 1/2 cup water. Allow to sit at room temperature for 12 hours, then repeat the feeding process.

Days 4-5-6 – Repeat the feeding process twice each day. By day 5 or 6 the starter should be strong enough to use in a loaf of bread. Signs that it is active enough include: nearly doubling in volume between feedings and slightly foamy at the surface. It should also have a strong, but pleasant acidic aroma.

BEFORE YOU BAKE

WHY MAKE HOME-MADE BREAD?

What are some reasons you may want to consider making your own bread?

One primary motivator for me is the elimination of any chemical preservatives, coloring, flavor, etc. that is often found in commercial breads. Even though there are many more whole grain options on the bread shelf, if the first ingredient in that bread doesn't say "100% whole wheat" or "100% whole grain," you can't be sure the product actually contains all three parts of whole grain (WebMD) and you may find a listing of numerous preservatives, flavor enhancers, etc.

Bread color is not a guarantee that the product is whole grain either. Many commercial breads contain artificial coloring. If "wheat flour" is not listed as a primary ingredient, it's likely that it was made with processed white flour.

Health benefits of whole grains include low in fat and cholesterol free; plant protein, loads of fiber, resistant starch, minerals vitamins, etc. When you make your own bread, you have much more control over the quality and freshness of the grain you use.

Commercial bakery-style breads made with authentic whole grain flavors and organic products are expensive. By making your own bread, you can use a store-brand organic all-purpose flour and produce a loaf of bread for around $3.00. Even if you make white bread, you can obtain organic flour and eliminate artificial flavor, color, and preservatives and make bread for about $2.00 per loaf.

In searching for flour sources, you may discover local or regional flour millers that can supply the types and quantities of flour you require at reasonable prices. Purchasing baking supplies from sources you know are reliable is valuable in itself.

Once you make homemade bread, you'll realize that the flavor, texture, and overall appeal of homemade bread makes it well worth the effort to make it at home. Today's bread makers and bread machines make bread baking so easy you may wonder why you didn't start baking bread sooner!

One other tool available to home bread makers today can make bread baking a simple task. The habit of warming bread recipe liquid (milk and water) to a temperature range between 105- and 110-degrees (Fahrenheit) almost guarantees a successful loaf time after time. Using a digital thermometer to verify the temperature of the liquid takes all the guess work out of it!

Pairing the precision of the digital thermometer with the efficiency of a bread machine – which thoroughly kneads the dough and stimulates the necessary gluten structure – gives bread makers the perfect "recipe" for baking success.

Once you're in the habit of baking your own bread, you'll find the economy of the bread makes it a sensible choice for making French toast, your own stuffing and bread crumbs, sweet rolls, dinner rolls, and more! If your goal is to master sourdough breads, the savings are even bigger. All of these products will also be free of added chemicals and preservatives, provide wonderfully fresh flavor, and add to your family's nutrition.

And don't dismiss the value of homemade bread as a gift! Baking bread at home has become more of a hobby, which the majority of people don't take up. So consider how you can provide someone with a tasty gift that's nutritious, healthy, and brings back fond memories of family times in the kitchen and at the dining room table.

Perhaps the question should be, "Why NOT make homemade bread?"

WHITE BREAD

With this recipe, you can use either all-purpose or bread flour. I prefer all-purpose flour. However, bread flour has added protein.

If you don't have a bread machine, you can still make this bread. Just know that the rise of the loaf and the texture of the bread is likely to be heavier than if you use a bread machine for the mixing and kneading.

BAKER'S TIP
Himalayan pink salt - covered by lava in the Himalaya - was naturally protected. Experts believe it is the purest salt that can be found on planet earth.

That's partly because your bread machine will maintain a more even heat for the dough in the canister than you could with a mixer. If mixing and kneading by hand, be sure to do so very thoroughly to properly develop the gluten, which is important to the rise, too.

1 cup water
1/3 cup milk
1 ½ teaspoons active dry yeast
¼ cup sugar, honey or maple syrup

3 ½ - 3 ¾ cups all-purpose or bread flour
1 ½ teaspoons salt

3 tablespoons of butter or oil

Use hot water out of the tap or warm the water within a temperature range of 105 to 110 degrees. Dissolve the sugar and milk in the water and check the temperature again. If it's below 105 degrees, warm it slightly on the stove top. Once the liquid is within the temperature range, dissolve the yeast in it and allow it to sit until the yeast is activated and bubbly.

While the yeast is activating, measure and mix the flour and salt. If using butter, cut into small pieces.

Once the yeast is ready, pour the mixture into the bread machine canister (or mixer bowl). Add the flour mixture and the butter/oil.

If you can program your bread machine, set it for these three cycles: 15 minutes mix/knead; 20 minutes rest; 10 minutes mix/knead. If you aren't able to program your machine, simply use a timer to work through the cycles. If you're using a mixer, the cycle times are exactly the same. Be sure to keep the dough covered and warm during the rest period. For each cycle, keep the mixer bowl and dough hook warm so it doesn't hamper your yeast action.

After the first five minutes of the initial mix/knead cycle, check the dough. If it sticks to your hand, it's too sticky. Add flour (2 tablespoons to 1/4 cup at a time) until the dough is moist but no longer sticks to your hand.

Once these three cycles are complete, prepare your bread pan by using non-stick spray, butter, oil, etc. You can shape the dough into a basic oblong roll. Cover the pan, place it in a warm location (i.e., the oven or stove top) and allow the dough to rise for 30 minutes.

Once the dough is risen to the top or slightly over the top of the pan, preheat the oven to 350 degrees and bake for 30 minutes. Cool on a rack and refrigerate once it's cooled.

BREAD FOR TWO

If you find that a two-pound loaf of bread is more than your family can use in one week, this one-pound loaf may be more suitable.

You can easily bake this loaf in a mini bread pan. But if you want standard-sized toast, sandwiches, etc., try using an 8.5x4.5 inch bread pan and block off the end of it to accommodate a shorter loaf.

To achieve a standard width on my loaf, I folded tin foil into a u-shape and tucked it into one end of my standard bread pan (8.5x4.5) My foil insert measured about 4.5x9 and folded down to 4.5 x 3x3x3 (3 long 3 high). The dough raised perfectly and gave me a really "cute" little loaf of bread!

To avoid using too much flour in this small loaf, I recommend using 1 ¾ cup to start with. Once you add the ingredients to the bread machine you can monitor the dough to determine if it's too sticky. If so, add flour using 1 or 2 tablespoons at a time to reach the desired consistency.

I created this recipe for my bread machine, but you don't have to have a bread machine to make it. Just follow directions for warming the milk and be sure to knead it thoroughly and then complete the final rise in a warm location.

½ cup milk
3 tablespoons sugar, honey or maple syrup
1 teaspoon active dry yeast

1 ¾-2 cups flour (either all-purpose or bread flour)
1/2 teaspoon salt

2 tablespoons butter, softened or chopped
1 egg, beaten (optional)

Warm milk to temperature range between 105 and 110 degrees. Mix in granulated sugar, stirringUse a digital thermometer to verify the temperature. to dissolve. Use a digital thermometer to verify temperature range is accurate. If it's less than 105, warm a small amount of the mixture and stir it back in to reach the proper temperature range. If it's too warm, allow it to cool. Once the temperature range is correct, add yeast, stirring to dissolve. Set the mixture aside for at least 3 minutes.

Sift flour and salt together. If including the egg (which adds flavor and supports a high rise), bring it to room temperature, then use a fork or small whisk to beat the egg.

Once the yeast is activated, pour the yeast mixture into your bread machine canister (you can warm the canister with hot water if your ambient temperatures are below 80 degrees Fahrenheit). Slowly add the flour mixture, then the beaten egg. Place the butter/oil on top of the flour.

If you can program your bread machine, set it for these three cycles: 15 minutes mix/knead; 20 minutes rest; 10 minutes mix/knead. If you aren't able to program your machine, simply use a timer to work through the cycles. If you're using a mixer, the cycle times are exactly the same. Be sure to keep the dough covered and warm during the rest period. For each cycle, keep the mixer bowl and dough hook warm so it doesn't hamper your yeast action.

After the first five minutes of the initial mix/knead cycle, check the dough. If it sticks to your hand, add flour (2 T – ¼ cup at a time) until the dough is moist but doesn't stick to your hand.

While the bread machine is working, prepare the foil insert. I folded foil into several layers to reach a 4.5-inch wide piece that was about 9 inches long. Folding it into the u-shape, tuck it into one end of your bread pan. Coat the rest of the pan with butter or a non-stick aerosol product.

When the dough is ready, form it into an oblong shape and place it into the pan. Cover the pan with a light cloth and allow it to rise in a warm location. It should reach a satisfactory raise in 30-45 minutes. Heat your oven to 350 degrees. and bake for 25-30 minutes.

EGG BREAD

You can certainly bake bread without using eggs. However, eggs are a rich source of protein that supplements gluten in flour and binds dough together. Adding eggs will enhance the rise of your dough and produce a soft, fluffy bread. As the bread bakes, the eggs will increase the browning of the crust. Eggs also add flavor to the bread and extend the shelf life of your loaf.

Why bother to bring the egg to room temperature before using it? Just like softened butter, the egg will blend more thoroughly into your dough if it's warmed. If necessary, allow the egg to sit in warm water for 10-15 minutes before you use it.

1 cup water
1/3 cup milk
1 ½ teaspoons active dry yeast
¼ cup sugar, honey or maple syrup

3 3/4 - 4 cups all-purpose or bread flour
1 ½ teaspoons salt
3 tablespoons of butter or oil

1 egg (at room temperature), slightly beaten

Use hot water out of the tap or warm the water within a temperature range of 105 to 110 degrees. Use a digital thermometer to verify the temperature. Dissolve the sugar and milk in the water and check the temperature again. If it's below 105 degrees, warm it slightly on the stove top. Once the liquid is within the temperature range, dissolve the yeast in it and allow it to sit until the yeast is activated and bubbly.

While the yeast is activating, measure and mix the flour and salt. If using butter, cut into small pieces.

Once the yeast is ready, pour the mixture into the bread machine

canister (or mixer bowl). Add the flour mixture and the butter/oil.

If you can program your bread machine, set it for these three cycles: 15 minutes mix/knead; 20 minutes rest; 10 minutes mix/knead. If you aren't able to program your machine, simply use a timer to work through the cycles. If you're using a mixer, the cycle times are exactly the same. Be sure to keep the dough covered and warm during the rest period. For each cycle, keep the mixer bowl and dough hook warm so it doesn't hamper your yeast action.

After the first five minutes of the initial mix/knead cycle, check the dough. If it sticks to your hand, it's too sticky. Add flour (2 tablespoons to 1/4 cup at a time) until the dough is moist but no longer sticks to your hand.

Once these three cycles are complete, prepare your bread pan by using non-stick spray, butter, oil, etc. You can shape the dough into a basic oblong roll. Cover the pan, place it in a warm location (i.e., the oven or stove top) and allow the dough to rise for 30 minutes.

Once the dough is risen to the top or slightly over the top of the pan, preheat the oven to 350 degrees and bake for 30 minutes. Cool on a rack and refrigerate once it's cooled.

OVERNIGHT DINNER ROLLS

This lovely dough will rest in your refrigerator overnight or for eight hours so you can have fresh bread with a meal. After removing it from the fridge, allow the dough to sit at room temperature for 45 minutes prior to baking.

While the yeast is activating, measure and mix the flour and salt. If using butter, cut it into pieces so it mixes easily into the dough.

Once the yeast is ready, pour the mixture into the bread machine canister (or mixer bowl). Add the flour, add the oil/butter.

In the bread machine, mix/knead these ingredients for 15 minutes (at slow speed on the mixer). If

you're using a mixer, be sure to keep the dough covered and warm during the rest period. Since you're not baking these rolls immediately, it's not as important to keep the dough warm as you mix/knead. The yeast will have time to grow slowly during the refrigeration period.

After the first five minutes of the initial mix/knead cycle, check the dough. If it sticks to your

> **BAKER'S TIP**
> Never allow the salt in your bread recipe to come into direct contact with your yeast, either before or after the yeast is activated. Salt kills yeast.

1 ½ teaspoon active dry yeast
1 1/3 cups water
¼ c sugar, honey or maple syrup
¼ cup oil or butter

1 ½ teaspoons salt
3 ½ cups flour
1 large egg, slightly beaten

Warm the water to a temperature range of 105 to 110 degrees. Use a digital thermometer to verify the temperature. Dissolve the sugar in the water and check the temperature again. If it's below 105, warm it slightly on the stove top. If it's too hot, allow it to cool to proper temperature range. Once the liquid is within the temperature range, dissolve the yeast in it and allow it to sit for about three minutes or until the yeast is activated and bubbly.

you can program your bread machine, set it for these two cycles: 15 minutes mix/knead; 20 minutes rest. If you aren't able to program your machine, simply use a timer to work through the cycles. If

hand, add all-purpose flour (2 tablespoons to ¼ cup at a time) until the dough is moist but doesn't stick to your hand.

Once these two cycles are complete, prepare your bread

pan by using non-stick spray, butter, oil, etc. Shape the dough into 20 balls and place them in the pan. Cover the pan with a bag or plastic wrap and store in the refrigerator overnight.

In the morning, or after eight hours, allow the dough to sit for 45 minutes before baking for 20-25 minutes in a preheated 375-degree oven. You want the rolls to be a nice, golden brown. Once they come out of the oven, immediately remove from the pan and, If desired, brush the rolls with melted butter.

As with any homemade bread, store in the refrigerator.

POTATO BREAD

Potato bread is soft and very moist. It makes wonderful toast and is a perfect complement to a meal. You can cook potatoes specifically for making the bread, use leftover potatoes, or potato flakes.

1 ½ teaspoons active dry yeast
2/3 cup water
1/4 cup sugar, honey or maple syrup

BAKER'S TIP
If you don't have access to high quality flour, adding an egg to your recipe will give your loaf a lift. You may need a few extra tablespoons of flour.

3-3 ½ cups flour (all-purpose or bread flour)
1 ½ teaspoons salt
½ cup cooked potatoes
(if using potato flakes, mix ½ cup with 1/3 cup water/milk)
3 tablespoons oil or butter
1 large egg

Warm the water to a temperature range of 105 to 110 degrees. Use a digital thermometer to verify the temperature. Dissolve the sugar in the water and check the temperature again. If it's too cool, warm it slightly on the stove top. Once the water is within the temperature range, dissolve the yeast in it and allow it to sit until the yeast is activated and bubbly.

While the yeast is activating, measure and mix the flour (3 cups to start with) and salt, then add the potatoes. Slightly beat the egg.

Once the yeast is ready, pour the mixture into the bread machine canister (or mixer bowl). Add the flour, oil/butter, and the egg.

If you can program your bread machine, set it for these three cycles: 15 minutes mix/knead; 20 minutes rest; 10 minutes mix/knead. If you aren't able to program your machine, simply use a timer to work through the cycles. If you're using a mixer, use the same times for these three cycles. In the mixer, be sure to keep the dough covered

and warm during the rest period. For each cycle, keep the mixer bowl and dough hook warm so it doesn't hamper your yeast action.

After the first five minutes of the initial mix/knead cycle, check the dough. If it sticks to your hand, add flour (2 T – ¼ cup at a time) until the dough is moist but doesn't stick to your hand.

Once these three cycles are complete, prepare your bread pan by using non-stick spray, butter, oil, etc. You can shape the dough into a basic oblong roll. Cover the pan, place it in a warm location (i.e. the oven or stove top) and allow the dough to rise for 30 minutes.

Once the dough is risen (up to or above the sides of the pan), preheat the oven to 350 degrees and bake for 30-40 minutes. Cool on a rack and refrigerate once it's cooled.

FLAX BREAD

Why is flax meal a good thing to add to your bread, at least sometimes? To begin with, the fat in flax is the heart-healthy omega 3 kind. Because it's an excellent source of dietary fiber, flax meal contributes to colon health. The protein in flax is similar to soybean protein and helps vegetarians meet daily protein requirements.

BAKER'S TIP
When adding ingredients like flax meal, your recipe may need a bit more liquid since the meal will absorb more liquid than flour would.

So here's a recipe to help you get started using flax meal in your home-made breads. You will love this bread!

1 1/4 cups water,
1/4 cup sugar, honey or maple syrup
1 1/2 teaspoons active dry yeast

3 1/4 to 3 1/2 cups 100% whole wheat flour (white wheat also works)
1/4 cup finely ground flax meal
1 1/2 teaspoons salt
3 tablespoons butter or oil

Warm the water to a temperature range of 105 to 110 degrees. Use a digital thermometer to verify the temperature. Dissolve the

sugar in the water and check the temperature again. If it's below 105 degrees, warm it slightly on the stove top. Once the water is within the temperature range, dissolve the yeast in it and allow it to sit until the yeast is activated and bubbly.

While the yeast is activating, measure and mix the flour, flax meal, and salt. If using butter, cut it into small pieces.

Once the yeast is ready, pour the mixture into the bread machine canister (or mixer bowl). Add the flour mixture and the butter/oil.

If you can program your bread machine, set it for these three cycles: 15 minutes mix/knead; 20 minutes rest; 10 minutes

mix/knead. If you aren't able to program your machine, simply use a timer to work through the cycles. If you're using a mixer, the cycle times are exactly the same. In the mixer, be sure to keep the dough covered and warm during the rest period. For each cycle, keep the mixer bowl and dough hook warm so it doesn't hamper your yeast action.

After the first five minutes of the initial mix/knead cycle, check the dough. If it sticks to your hand, add flour (2 tablespoons to ¼ cup at a time) until the dough is moist but doesn't stick to your hand.

Once these three cycles are complete, prepare your bread pan by using non-stick spray, butter, oil, etc. You can shape the dough into a basic oblong roll.

Cover the pan, place it in a warm location (i.e. the oven or stove top) and allow the dough to rise for 30 minutes.

Once the dough is risen to the top or slightly over the top of the pan, preheat the oven to 350 degrees and bake for 30 minutes. Cool on a rack and refrigerate once it's cooled.

FRENCH BREAD

If you've never tried making your own French bread, you'll be pleased to f ind how easy it is. See the information in the front of the book about how to use a couche or a baguette pan to obtain the desired loaf shape.

1 ½ cups water
1 tablespoon sugar, honey or maple syrup
1 ½ teaspoons active dry yeast

BAKER'S TIP
You don't necessarily need a special pan or baker's couche to make the bread. Just shape it and use a foil "bed" to help hold the shape while it rises.

4 to 5 cups all-purpose flour (could use whole wheat or white wheat)
2 teaspoons salt
1 tablespoon butter or oil

Warm the water to a temperature range of 105 to 110 degrees. Use a digital thermometer to verify the temperature. Dissolve the sugar in the water and check the temperature again. If it's below 105, warm it slightly on the stove top. If it's too hot, allow it to cool. Once the water is within the temperature range, dissolve the yeast in it and allow it to sit until the yeast is activated and bubbly.

While the yeast is activating, measure and mix the flour and salt. If using butter, cut into small pieces.

Once the yeast is ready, pour the mixture into the bread machine canister (or mixer bowl). Add the flour mixture and the butter.

Mix the dough in the bread machine or mixer until it's smooth, approximately 5 minutes. Do not knead! Cover the dough and a let it rise in a warm place until it's doubled, about 30 minutes.

Turn onto a floured surface. Divide the dough in half and allow it to rest for 10 minutes. Roll each half into a 10x8-inch rectangle. Roll up from a long

side; pinch to seal. You can use a baguette pan or baker's couche (a piece of flax cloth) to raise these loaves. Cover and allow to rise for about 30 minutes.

When it's ready to bake, with a very sharp knife or lame`, make 5 diagonal cuts across the top of each loaf. If using a baguette pan, set it right in the oven. If using a couche, roll the loaves onto a baking sheet and bake at 400 degrees for 20 to 30 minutes, until lightly browned. Remove from pans to wire rack to cool.

CHEESE BREAD

This bread smells so good while it's baking that I wish I could purchase a fragrance or room deodorizer that mimics the smell! You will see fragments of the cheese in the bread, flecks of onion salt in the crust, and you'll watch this loaf disappear like magic once your family gets their hands on it!

BAKER'S TIP
Avoid the temptation to increase cheese amount for this bread. If you prefer a stronger cheese flavor, use a stronger-flavored cheese variety.

1 cup water
1 tablespoon active dry yeast
¼ cup sugar, honey or maple syrup

3 ¾ - 4 cups all-purpose or bread flour
1 ½ teaspoons salt
1-2 tablespoons caraway seed (optional)
½ tablespoon onion salt

1 egg, lightly beaten

3 tablespoons butter or oil

1 cup grated sharp cheddar cheese

Warm the water to a temperature range of 105 to 110 degrees. Use a digital thermometer to verify the temperature. Dissolve the sugar in the water and check the temperature again. If it's less than 105 degrees, warm it slightly on the stove top. If it's too hot, allow it to cool. Once the water is within the temperature range, dissolve the yeast in it and allow it to sit until the yeast is activated and bubbly.

While the yeast is activating, measure and mix the flour, salt, caraway seed, and onion salt. If using butter, cut it into small pieces.

Once the yeast is ready, pour the mixture into the bread machine canister (or mixer bowl). Add the

flour mixture and the butter.

If you can program your bread machine, set it for these three cycles: 15 minutes mix/knead; 20 minutes rest; 10 minutes mix/knead. If you aren't able to program your machine, simply use a timer to work through the cycles. If you're using a mixer, the cycle times are exactly the same. Be sure to keep the dough covered and warm during the rest period. For each cycle, keep the mixer bowl and dough hook warm so it doesn't hamper your yeast action.

After the first five minutes of the initial mix/knead cycle, check the dough. If it sticks to your hand, add flour (2 tablespoons to ¼ cup at a time) until the dough is moist but no longer sticks to your hand.

Whether you use a bread machine or a mixer, add the grated cheese five minutes before the final mix/knead cycle ends.

Once these three cycles are complete, prepare your bread pan by using non-stick spray, butter, oil, etc. Shape the dough into a basic oblong roll. Cover the pan, place it in a warm location (i.e. the oven or stove top) and allow the dough to rise for 30 minutes.

Once the dough is risen to the top or slightly over the top of the pan, preheat the oven to 350 degrees and bake for 30 minutes. Cool on a rack and refrigerate once it's cooled.

HERBED BREAD

This recipe infuses herbal flavors into a light, fluffy loaf of bread. And you can use this loaf to make stuffing mix, croutons, etc.

1 cup water
1/3 cup milk
1 ½ teaspoons active dry yeast
¼ cup sugar, honey or maple syrup

BAKER'S TIP
To measure flour, use a scoop to fill your cup to ensure you're not packing flour into the cup.

---

3 ½ - 3 ¾ cups all-purpose or bread flour
1 ½ teaspoons salt

3 tablespoons of butter or oil

1 teaspoon dried sage
2 teaspoons dried basil
2 teaspoons dried oregano
1 teaspoon thyme

Mix the milk and water and warm it to a temperature range of 105 to 110 degrees. Use a digital thermometer to verify the temperature. Dissolve the sugar in the liquid and check the temperature again. If it's less than 105, warm it slightly on the stove top. Once the water is

within the temperature range, dissolve the yeast in it and allow it to sit until the yeast is activated and bubbly.

While the yeast is activating, measure and mix the flour, salt, and herbs. If using butter, cut it into small pieces.

Once the yeast is ready, pour the mixture into the bread machine canister (or mixer bowl). Add the flour mixture and the butter/oil.

If you can program your bread machine, set it for these three cycles: 15 minutes mix/knead; 20 minutes rest; 10 minutes mix/knead. If you aren't able to

program your machine, simply use a timer to work through the cycles. If you're using a mixer, the cycle times are exactly the same. Be sure to keep the dough covered and warm during the rest period. For each cycle, keep the mixer bowl and dough hook warm so it doesn't hamper your yeast action.

After the first five minutes of the initial mix/knead cycle, check the dough. If it sticks to your hand, add flour (2 tablespoons to ¼ cup at a time) until the dough is moist but doesn't stick to your hand.

Once these three cycles are complete, prepare your bread pan by using non-stick spray, butter, oil, etc. You can shape the dough into a basic oblong roll. Cover the pan, place it in a warm location (i.e. the oven or stove top) and allow the dough to rise for 30 minutes.

Once the dough is risen to the top or slightly over the top of the pan, preheat the oven to 350 degrees and bake for 30 minutes. Cool on a rack and refrigerate once it's cooled.

STUFFING MIX

Whether you need stuffing mix, croutons, bread crumbs, or your bread has become dry and stale and you don't want to just throw it away, you can make all three of these foods very easily.

You may not have a lot of bread left over very often, in which case you can bake some bread just for use as crumbs, stuffing, etc. You can also recycle a loaf that didn't rise very well or was otherwise unsatisfactory.

> **BAKER'S TIP**
> Stale or botched bread can be recycled in numerous ways, including making bread crumbs that you could add to your next batch of dough.

BREADCRUMBS
There's no need to dry your bread before breaking it down for breadcrumbs. It's actually easier and faster to crumble the bread and then dry it. You can use scraps that are left over or use an entire loaf to build up a stash of breadcrumbs.

If you crumble a large amount of bread to make crumbs, you'll want to spread the crumbs out in a bread pan or a cookie sheet and set them in a 200-degree oven for an hour or two to dry. If you use the oven, allow the crumbs to cool after you take them out of the oven before storing them in an airtight container. I recommend labeling the container somewhere with a date, unless you expect to quickly use them up.

CROUTONS
Thickly sliced bread
Olive oil
Seasonings as desired to include: Garlic salt, onion salt, salt, pepper, red pepper flakes, etc/

1. Preheat the oven to 400 degrees.
2. Cut the bread into cubes and place in a large bowl. Drizzle cubes with olive oil and seasonings. Mix well.
3. Spread the bread out on a sheet pan and bake for about 15 minutes.
4. Allow to cool and thoroughly dry before storing in an airtight container such as a jar or plastic bag.

STUFFING MIX
½ cup plus 1 tablespoon dried celery flakes
3 tablespoons dried minced onion
3 tablespoons dried parsley flakes
2 tablespoons chicken bouillon granules
1 ½ teaspoons poultry seasoning
¾ teaspoon rubbed sage
10 cups dried bread cubes (approximately 24 slices)

1 cup water
2 tablespoons butter

1. Crumble the bread and spread out in a pan or on a cookie sheet and place in a 200-degree oven to dry. Remove from the oven and allow to cool before mixing with the seasonings.
2. Combine the first six ingredients.
3. Mix with the breadcrumbs.
4. Make sure the bread is thoroughly dry before storing in an airtight container.

To use the stuffing mix:
1 cup water
2 tablespoons butter

Heat the water and butter and bring to a boil. Reduce heat, add 1/3 cup of stuffing mix, cover and simmer for 10 minutes. Remove from heat and allow to stand for 5 minutes, fluff with a fork and serve.

You can also use the Herbed Bread recipe in this book to make stuffing mix or croutons. The Cheddar Cheese Bread and Flax Bread also make delicious croutons.

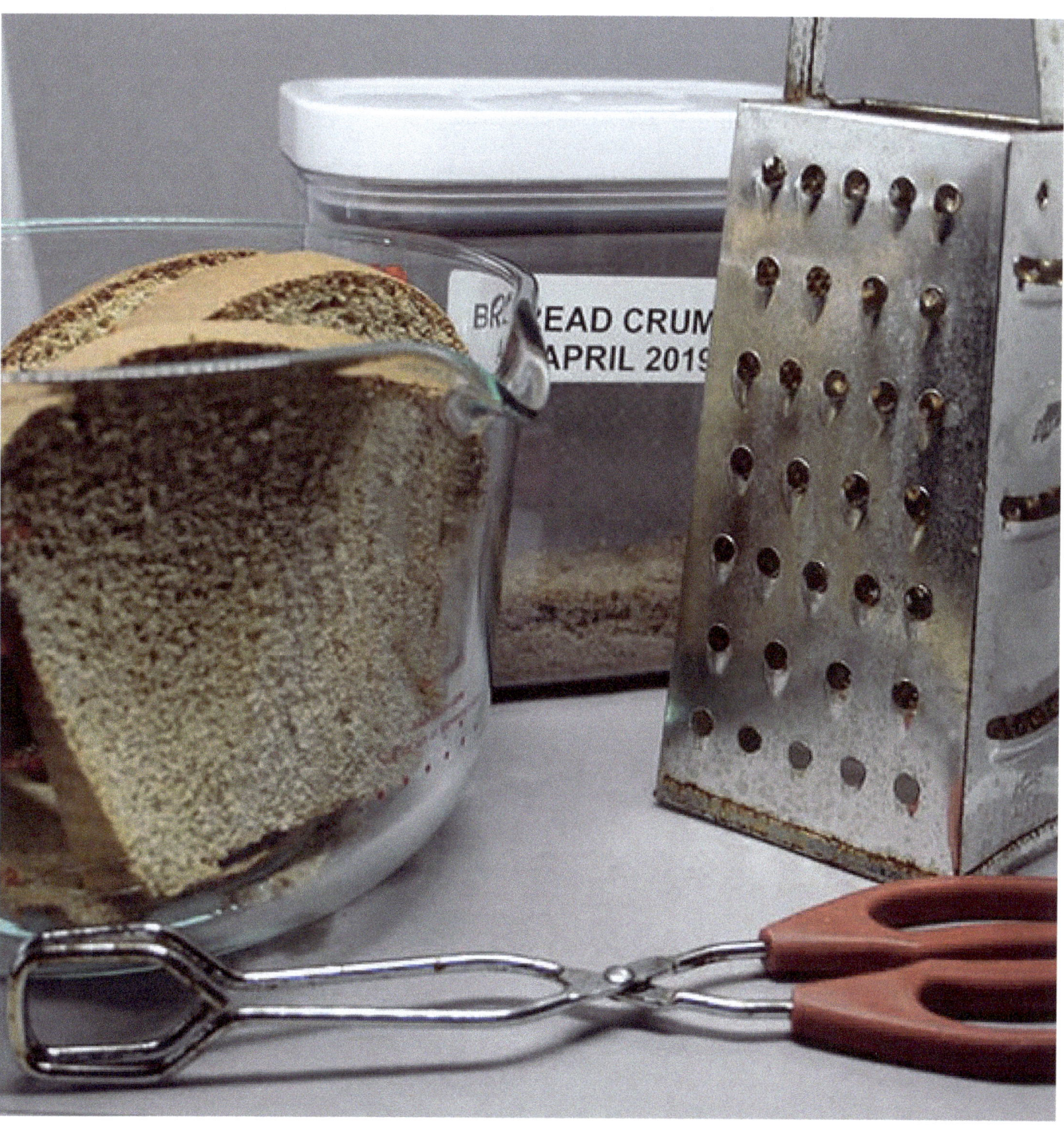

HERBED BREAD STICKS

We love the herbed flavor of these bread sticks, but you could make them without the herbs. If you eliminate the herbs, do include the garlic and onion seasonings. You can mix the herbs and seasonings into the dough or sprinkle them on top of the sticks just

1 1/3 cups water
1/4 cup dry milk powder
2 teaspoons active dry yeast
¼ cup sugar, honey or maple syrup

4 cups all-purpose or bread flour
1 ½ teaspoons salt
2 tablespoons sugar

2 tablespoons grated parmesan cheese
1 teaspoon garlic powder
1 teaspoon garlic salt
1 tablespoon onion powder
1 tablespoon dried oregano
1 teaspoon dried basil

3 tablespoons of butter or oil

2 tablespoons melted butter to brush on baked sticks

Warm the water to a temperature range of 105 to 110 degrees. Use a digital thermometer to verify the temperature. Dissolve the sugar in the water and check the temperature again. If it's below 105 degrees, warm it slightly on the stove top. Once the water is within the temperature range, dissolve the yeast in it and allow it to sit until the yeast is activated and bubbly.

While the yeast is activating, measure and mix the flour, seasonings, and salt. If using butter, cut it into small pieces.

Once the yeast is ready, pour the mixture into the bread machine canister (or mixer bowl). Add the flour mixture and the butter/oil.

If you can program your bread machine, set it for these three cycles: 15 minutes mix/knead; 20 minutes rest; 10 minutes mix/knead. If you aren't able to program your machine, simply use a timer to work through the cycles. If you're using a mixer, the cycle times are exactly the same. Be sure to keep the dough covered and warm during the rest period. For each cycle, keep the mixer bowl and dough hook warm so it doesn't hamper your yeast action.

After the first five minutes of the initial mix/knead cycle, check the dough. If it sticks to your hand, add flour (2 tablespoons to ¼ cup at a time) until the dough is moist but no longer sticks to your hand.

Once these three cycles are complete, prepare two 9x11 pans by laying a sheet of parchment paper across the bottom of each pan. To shape the sticks, pinch off dough as you would to make dinner rolls. Shape into a rope-like oblong piece of dough. Cover the pans, place them in a warm location (i.e. the oven or stove top) and allow the dough to rise for 30 minutes.

Once the dough is risen, preheat the oven to 450 degrees and bake for 10-15 minutes. Keep an eye on these as they will quickly brown and could easily scorch if baked too long. Cool on a rack and refrigerate or freeze the sticks once they have cooled.

PARMESAN BREADSTICKS

Combining these two flavors in a bread stick makes a heavenly bread to accompany pizza, spaghetti, chili soup, etc. And using the bread machine to develop the dough makes it an easy process.

3/4 cups water
1/4 cup milk
¼ cup sugar
2 teaspoons active dry yeast

> **BAKER'S TIP**
> How are breadsticks shaped? That's all up to you. Make them as small or as larage as you would like. Use a pizza cutter to cut your dough.

2 1/4 – 2 1/2 cups flour
1 teaspoon salt

½ teaspoon minced garlic
½ cup grated parmesan cheese
½ teaspoon garlic salt
¾ teaspoon dried Italian seasoning

4 tablespoons of butter or oil

2 tablespoons melted butter to brush on baked sticks

Warm the water to a temperature range of 105 to 110 degrees. Use a digital thermometer to verify the temperature. Dissolve sugar and milk (or milk powder) in the water and check the temperature again. If it's below 105 degrees, warm it slightly on the stove top. Once the water is within the temperature range, dissolve the yeast in it and allow it to sit until the yeast is activated and bubbly.

While the yeast is activating, measure and mix the flour, seasonings (unless you're sprinkling on top of the sticks), and salt. Cut the butter into small pieces.

Once the yeast is ready, pour the mixture into the bread machine canister (or mixer bowl). Add the flour mixture and the butter.

If you can program your bread machine, set it for these three cycles: 15 minutes mix/knead;

20 minutes rest; 10 minutes mix/knead. If you aren't able to program your machine, simply use a timer to work through the cycles. If you're using a mixer, the cycle times are exactly the same. Be sure to keep the dough covered and warm during the rest period. For each cycle, keep the mixer bowl and dough hook warm so it doesn't hamper your yeast action.

After the first five minutes of the initial mix/knead cycle, check the dough. If it sticks to your hand, add flour (2 tablespoons to ¼ cup at a time) until the dough is moist but no longer sticks to your hand.

Once these three cycles are complete, prepare two 9x11 pans by laying a sheet of parchment paper across the bottom of each pan. To shape the sticks, pinch off dough as you would to make dinner rolls. Shape into a rope-like oblong piece of dough. Cover the pans, place them in a warm location (i.e. the oven or stove top) and allow the dough to rise for 30 minutes.

Once the dough is risen, preheat the oven to 450 degrees and bake for 10-15 minutes. Keep an eye on these as they will quickly brown and could easily scorch if baked too long. Cool on a rack and refrigerate or freeze the sticks once they have cooled.

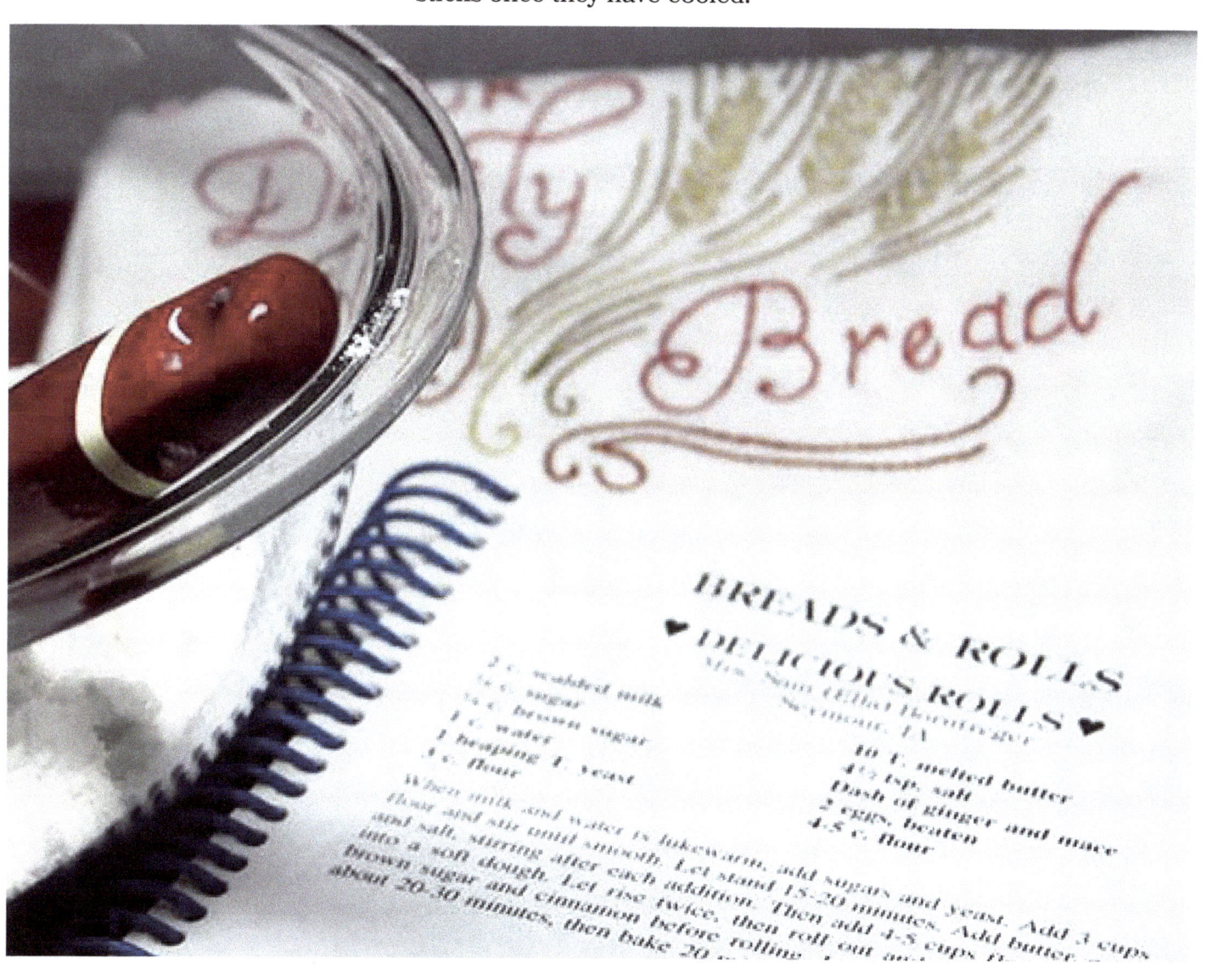

PIZZA DOUGH

We like garlic flavor in our pizza, and I use both garlic salt and garlic powder in this recipe. If you're not fond of that flavor, you can certainly omit or substitute for taste preferences. We also prefer a thinner crust. If you like thick crust pizza, use the recipe for two pizza doughs to make a pizza crust for a 9x13 pan or 12-inch round pan. This dough is moist and soft and bakes up as a well-browned pizza crust.

BAKER'S TIP
You can make your pizza crust as thick or thin as you like. For crispy crust, pre-bake for 5-10 minutes before adding pizza toppings.

The easiest way to make this dough is with a bread machine, but you can also use a mixer with a dough hook. In the mixer, warm the mixer bowl and dough hook to help keep the dough warm and support yeast action.

One 12-inch pizza dough:
½ cup water
2 tablespoons sugar
¾ teaspoon active dry yeast

1 ½ c flour
2 teaspoons garlic salt
2 teaspoons garlic powder
1 teaspoon Italian seasoning
¼ cup grated Parmesan cheese
1 tablespoon garlic bread sprinkle w/cheese
3 tablespoons olive oil or butter

Two 12-inch pizza doughs:
1 cup water
¼ cup sugar
1 ½ teaspoons active dry yeast

3 – 3 1/2 cups flour
2 teaspoons garlic salt
2 teaspoons garlic powder
1 teaspoon Italian seasoning
½ cup grated Parmesan cheese
2 tablespoons garlic bread sprinkle
2 tablespoons olive oil or butter

Warm the water to a temperature range between 105 and 110 degrees. Use a digital thermometer to verify the temperature. Dissolve the sugar in the water and recheck the temperature. If it's less than 105, warm it slightly on the stove

top. Once the temperature is accurate, dissolve the yeast and allow it to activate and become bubbly.

While the yeast activates, measure and mix the flour and salt. If using butter, cut it into small pieces.

If you can program your bread machine, set it for these three cycles: 15 minutes mix/knead; 20 minutes rest; 10 minutes mix/knead. If you aren't able to program your machine, simply use a timer to work through the cycles. If you're using a mixer, the cycle times are exactly the same. Be sure to keep the dough covered and warm during the rest period. For each cycle, keep the mixer bowl and dough hook warm so it doesn't hamper your yeast action.

After the first five minutes of the initial mix/knead cycle, check the dough. If it sticks to your hand, add flour (2 tablespoons to ¼ cup at a time) until the dough is moist but no longer sticks to your hand.

At the end of the last cycle, place the dough on a lightly floured work surface. If making two pizza crusts, divide the dough into two equal pieces. Press down and roll out each piece into the desired shape for your pizza pan. Spread the garlic bread sprinkle evenly across the dough. Add more or less, according to taste preference.

Allow the dough to rise for 20-30 minutes. Assemble your pizza and bake at 400 degrees for 20-25 minutes.

WHITE WHEAT BREAD

White wheat is a whole grain, but it's color and flavor are less intense than traditional whole wheat varieties. For this reason, white wheat bread is often more readily accepted by those who don't like the characteristics of 100% whole wheat bread. In some cases, you may barely be able to tell it's a whole grain. This loaf will have small specs of the milled grain, but it will look very much like a loaf of white bread.

1 1/4 cups water
1 ½ teaspoons active dry yeast
¼ cup sugar, honey or maple syrup

3 ½ - 4 cups 100% white wheat flour
1 ½ teaspoons salt

3 tablespoons of butter or oil

Warm the water to a temperature range of 105 to 110 degrees. Use a digital thermometer to verify the temperature. Dissolve the sugar in the water and check the temperature again. If it's below 105, warm it slightly on the stove top. Once the water is within the temperature range, dissolve the yeast in it and allow it to sit until the yeast is activated and bubbly.

While the yeast is activating, measure and mix the flour and salt. If using butter, cut it into small pieces.

Once the yeast is ready, pour the mixture into the bread machine canister (or mixer bowl). Add the flour mixture and the butter/oil.

If you can program your bread machine, set it for these three cycles: 15 minutes mix/knead; 20 minutes rest; 10 minutes mix/knead. If you aren't able to program your machine, simply use a timer to work through the cycles. If you're using a mixer, the cycle times are exactly the same. Be sure to keep the dough covered and warm during the rest.

After the first five minutes of the initial mix/knead cycle, check the dough. If it sticks to your hand, add flour (2 tablespoons to ¼ cup at a time) until the dough is moist but no longer sticks to your hand.

Once these three cycles are complete, prepare your bread pan by using non-stick spray, butter, oil, etc. You can shape the dough into a basic oblong roll. Cover the pan, place it in a warm location (i.e. the oven or stove top) and allow the dough to rise for 30 minutes.

After the dough is risen to the top or slightly over the top of the pan, preheat the oven to 350 degrees and bake for 30 minutes. Cool on a wire rack and refrigerate once it's cooled.

WHOLE WHEAT BREAD

If you're tired of making brick-like whole wheat loaves of bread, I have good news for you!

Here is a recipe and method which will give you the light, tasty, whole wheat loaf you've been dreaming about.

With this recipe, you can use any type of 100% whole wheat flour (I prefer organic) or even grind your own flour from wheat berries.

BAKER'S TIP
Always store your whole grain flours in the refrigerator or freezer so the oils in them won't become rancid.

If you don't have a bread machine, you can still make this bread. However, the rise of the loaf and the texture of the bread is likely to be heavier than if you use a bread machine for the mixing and kneading. If mixing and kneading by hand, be sure to do so very thoroughly.

1 ¼ cups water
1 ½ teaspoons active dry yeast
¼ cup sugar, honey or maple syrup

3 ½ - 4 cups 100% whole wheat flour
1 ½ teaspoons salt

2 tablespoons of melted butter or oil

Warm the water to a temperature range of 105 to 110 degrees. Use a digital thermometer to verify the temperature. Dissolve the sugar in the water and check the temperature again. If it's below 105, warm it slightly on the stove top. Once the water is within the temperature range, dissolve the yeast in it and allow it to sit until the yeast is activated and bubbly.

While the yeast is activating, measure and mix the flour and salt. If using butter, cut it into small pieces.

Once the yeast is ready, pour the mixture into the bread machine canister (or mixer bowl). Add the flour mixture and the butter/oil.

If you can program your bread machine, set it for these three cycles: 15 minutes mix/knead; 20 minutes rest; 10 minutes mix/knead. If you aren't able to program your machine, simply use a timer to work through the cycles. If you're using a mixer, the cycle times are exactly the same. Be sure to keep the dough covered and warm during the rest period. For each cycle, keep the mixer bowl and dough hook warm so it doesn't hamper your yeast action.

After the first five minutes of the initial mix/knead cycle, check the dough. If it sticks to your hand, add flour (2 tablespoons to ¼ cup at a time) until the dough is moist but no longer sticks to your hand.

Once these three cycles are complete, prepare your bread pan by using non-stick spray, butter, oil, etc. You can shape the dough into a basic oblong roll. Cover the pan, place it in a warm location (i.e. the oven or stove top) and allow the dough to rise for 30 minutes.

Once the dough is risen to the top or slightly over the top of the pan, preheat the oven to 350 degrees and bake for 30 minutes. Cool on a wire rack and refrigerate once it's cooled.

ENGLISH MUFFINS

If you've never tried making English muffins, you're in for a treat. Use either white, white wheat, or a combination of the two and enjoy right out of the skillet!

1 ½ cups milk
¼ c sugar, honey or maple syrup
2 teaspoons dry active yeast
3 T. Butter
2 cups white flour (bread flour optional)
2 cups whole wheat flour
1 ½ teaspoons salt

> **BAKER'S TIP**
> English muffins can be cooked in a standard frying pan. When warm, outside edges may appear to be doughy but 5 minutes per side is adequate cook time.

Heat the milk to a temperature range between 105 and 110 degrees. Use a digital thermometer to verify the temperature. Dissolve the sugar and check the temperature again. If it's less than 105, heat the liquid on the stove top for a few minutes, or heat 2-3 tablespoons of liquid and add back into the mixture. Once the desired temperature range is reached, dissolve the yeast and set the mixture aside so the yeast can activate.

Blend the flours and salt. Cut the butter into small pieces so it easily blends into the dough.

If you can program your bread machine, set it for these three cycles: 15 minutes mix/knead; 20 minutes rest; 10 minutes mix/knead. If you aren't able to program your machine, simply use a timer to work through the cycles. If you're using a mixer, the cycle times are exactly the same. Be sure to keep the dough covered and warm during the rest period. For each cycle, keep the mixer bowl and dough hook warm so it doesn't hamper your yeast action.

After the first five minutes of the initial mix/knead cycle, check the dough. If it sticks to your hand, add flour (2 tablespoons to ¼ cup at a time) until the dough is moist but doesn't stick to your hand.

Once these three cycles are complete, roll the dough out to about ½ inch thick. Using a floured 3-inch biscuit cutter or the floured rim of a glass, cut out 9-12 muffins. If desired, reroll the trimmings and cut out one or two more muffins.

Place the muffins on a baking sheet or inside muffin rings, dust with semolina flour (optional), and cover with oiled plastic wrap. Allow the muffins to rise in a warm place for 20 minutes, or until nearly doubled in size.

Heat a griddle over a medium heat and oil it lightly with non-stick spray or olive oil. Cook the muffins slowly, at a heat between medium and low, for about 5 minutes on each side. Cool on a rack.

SWEDISH RYE BREAD

1 ½ teaspoons active dry yeast
1 1/3 cups water
¼ cup packed brown sugar

1 ¼ cup rye flour
2 to 2 ¼ cups flour (all-purpose or bread flour)
2 tablespoons molasses
2 tablespoons oil or butter
1 ½ teaspoons salt

1 tablespoon melted butter (optional for brushing on baked loaf)

> **BAKER'S TIP**
> Rye bread is sometimes favored because it's lower in gluten than other grains. However, it's not suitable for a gluten-free diet.

Rye flour has less gluten than wheat flour, which causes it to be a denser loaf. Using the proper temperature for the recipe liquid and kneading the dough adequately with either a bread machine or mixer with dough hook will help optimize the rise and lightness of this loaf.

Warm the water to a temperature range of 105 to 110 degrees. Use a digital thermometer to verify the temperature. Dissolve the sugar in the water and check the temperature again. If it's less than 105, warm it slightly on the stove top. If it's too warm, allow it to cool. Once the liquid is within the temperature range, dissolve the yeast in it and allow it to sit until the yeast is activated and bubbly.

While the yeast is activating, measure and mix the flour and salt. If using butter, cut it into several pieces so it mixes easily into the dough.

Once the yeast is ready, pour the mixture into the bread machine canister (or mixer bowl). Add the flour, add the oil/butter, and the molasses.

If you can program your bread machine, set it for these three cycles: 15 minutes mix/knead; 20 minutes rest; 10 minutes mix/knead. If you aren't able to program your machine, simply use a timer to work through the cycles. If you're using a mixer, be sure to keep the dough covered and warm during the rest period. For each cycle, keep the mixer bowl and dough hook warm so it doesn't hamper yeast action.

After the first five minutes of the initial mix/knead cycle, check the dough. If it sticks to your hand, add flour (2 tablespoons to ¼ cup at a time) until the dough is moist but doesn't stick to your hand.

Once these three cycles are complete, prepare your bread pan by using non-stick spray, butter, oil, etc. You can shape the dough into a basic oblong roll. This dough will feel heavy and perhaps more dry than a white-bread dough. Cover the pan, place it in a warm location (i.e. the oven or stove top) and allow the dough to rise for 30 to 40 minutes, until the dough reaches at or slightly above the top of the pan. Rye bread dough may sometimes require a longer rising period than white bread.

After the dough has raised (up to or above the sides of the pan), preheat the oven to 350 degrees and bake for 30-40 minutes. Cool on a rack and refrigerate once it's cooled.

RUSSIAN BLACK BREAD

This beautiful bread has a rich, whole grain reflects the flavors of the cocoa, coffee and molasses in the recipe. It's similar to pumpernickel bread, without the strong molasses tang.

If you don't have a bread machine, you can still make this bread. However, the rise of the loaf and texture of the bread is likely to be heavier than if you use a bread machine for the mixing and kneading.

BAKER'S TIP
When you pair a dark bread like this with cheese slices or cheese spread, you will enjoy a heavenly treat!

If mixing and kneading by hand, be sure to do so very thoroughly.

1 ½ cups water
2 teaspoons dry active yeast
¼ cup sugar, honey or maple syrup

2 ¼- 2 3/4 cups all-purpose or bread flour
1 ¼ cups rye flour
3/4 cup whole wheat (or white wheat) flour
3/4 cup dried bread crumbs
2 teaspoons salt
1 ½ tablespoons cocoa powder
2 ½ tablespoons instant coffee granules
1 ½ teaspoons caraway seeds (optional)
4 tablespoons butter or oil

1 egg at room temperature (optional)
2 ½ tablespoons molasses

Warm the water to a temperature range of 105 to 110 degrees. Use a digital thermometer to verify the temperature. Dissolve the sugar in the water and check the temperature again. If it's less than 105, warm it slightly on the stove top. If it's too warm allow it to cool. Once the water is within the temperature range, dissolve the yeast in it and allow it to sit until the yeast is activated and bubbly.

While the yeast activates, measure and mix the flours, salt, bread crumbs, cocoa powder,

and coffee granules Cut the butter into small pieces.

Once the yeast is ready, pour the mixture into the bread machine canister (or mixer bowl). Add the flour mixture and the butter/oil.

If you can program your bread machine, set it for these three cycles: 15 minutes mix/knead; 20 minutes rest; 10 minutes mix/knead. If you aren't able to program your machine, simply use a timer to work through the cycles. If you're using a mixer, the cycle times are exactly the same. Be sure to keep the dough covered and warm during the rest period. For each cycle, keep the mixer bowl and dough hook warm so it doesn't hamper your yeast action.

After the first five minutes of the initial mix/knead cycle, check the dough. If it sticks to your hand, add flour (2 tablespoons to ¼ cup at a time) until the dough is moist but doesn't stick to your hand.

Once these three cycles are complete, prepare your bread pan by using non-stick spray, butter, oil, etc. You can shape the dough into a basic oblong roll. Cover the pan, place it in a warm location (i.e. the oven or stove top) and allow the dough to rise for 30 to 40 minutes.

After the dough is risen to the top or slightly over the top of the pan, preheat the oven to 350 degrees and bake for 30 minutes. Cool on a rack and refrigerate once it's cooled.

PUMPERNICKEL BREAD

I love to bake this bread in the form of mini loaves, which makes each slice a perfect snack when paired with cheese. The pleasing flavor of pumpernickel bread comes from the combination of molasses and caraway seed. These loaves freeze beautifully so you always have some on hand when company drops by.

BAKER'S TIP
To obtain a stonger flavor for this bread, increase the amount of rye flour and/or molasses.

¾ cup water
1 ½ teaspoons active dry yeast
2 tablespoons sugar, honey or maple syrup

1 cup all-purpose or bread flour
1/3 cup rye flour
1/3 cup whole wheat flour (or white wheat)
1 teaspoon salt
2 tablespoons cornmeal
5 teaspoons cocoa powder
3 teaspoons dry milk powder
1 teaspoon caraway seeds
¼ teaspoon instant coffee granules

2 tablespoons molasses
3 tablespoons butter/oil

Warm the water to a temperature range of 105 to 110 degrees. Use a digital thermometer to verify the temperature. Dissolve the sweetener in the water and check the temperature again. If it's less than 105, warm it slightly on the stove top. Once the water is within the temperature range, dissolve the yeast in it and allow it to sit until the yeast is activated and bubbly.

While the yeast is activating, measure and mix the flours, salt, cornmeal, cocoa, milk powder, coffee granules, and caraway seed. If using butter, cut it into small pieces.

Once the yeast is ready, pour the mixture into the bread machine canister (or mixer bowl). Add the flour mixture, the butter/oil, and the molasses.

If you can program your bread machine, set it for these three cycles: 15 minutes mix/knead; 20 minutes rest; 10 minutes mix/knead. If you aren't able to program your machine, simply use a timer to work through the cycles. If you're using a mixer, the cycle times are exactly the same. Be sure to keep the dough covered and warm during the rest period. For each cycle, keep the mixer bowl and dough hook warm so it doesn't hamper your yeast action.

After the first five minutes of the initial mix/knead cycle, check the dough. If it sticks to your hand, add flour (2 tablespoons to ¼ cup at a time) until the dough is moist but no longer sticks to your hand.

Once these three cycles are complete, prepare your bread pan by using non-stick spray, butter, oil, etc. You can shape the dough into a basic oblong roll. Cover the pan, place it in a warm location (i.e. the oven or stove top) and allow the dough to rise for 30 to 40 minutes.

Once the dough is risen to the top or slightly over the top of the pan, preheat the oven to 350 degrees and bake for 30 minutes. Cool on a rack and refrigerate once it's cooled.

EZEKIEL BREAD

I could probably write an entire book about the wonderful flavor and nutrition fourd in this recipe, entirely an original that came out of my research and experimentation with different flour combinations. The ingredients are those found in the book of Ezekiel, chapter 4, verse 9. With this recipe, you'll produce a hearty, high-rising, nutrition loaf of bread that, in my opinion, outshines any other type of bread I've ever made.

BAKER'S TIP
The ingredients in this Ezekiel bread recipe make it highly nutritious and high in protein.

Medium Loaf

The taste of this bread is divine whether you make toast, sandwiches, or simply layer it with honey or jam. You won't believe how easy it is to make this. Don't miss the Ezekiel Bread Mix recipe, which will make it even easier to provide your family with this outstanding loaf. It's well worth it to keep white wheat flour (or white wheat berries) on hand as regular whole wheat bread will produce a slightly heavier loaf and alter the superb taste of this loaf.

It's helpful to grind (or purchase) your flours ahead of time. Depending on how often you plan to make this loaf, you won't need a large volume of any of the specialty flours the recipe calls for.

1 ½ teaspoons active dry yeast
1 1/4 cup water
¼ cup honey, or maple syrup, or sugar

1 ½ teaspoons salt
2 ¼ cups white wheat flour
¾ cups spelt flour
¼ cup barley flour
¼ cup millet flour
¼ cup lentil flour
¼ cup bean flour (black bean is preferable)

3 tablespoons oil or butter

Warm the water to a temperature range of 105 to 110 degrees. Use

a digital thermometer to verify the temperature. Dissolve the sweetener in the water and check the temperature again. If it's less than 105, warm it slightly on the stove top. If it's too warm, allow it to cool. Once the liquid is within the temperature range, dissolve the yeast in it and allow it to sit for about three minutes or until the yeast is activated and bubbly.

While the yeast is activating, measure and mix the flours and salt. If using butter, cut it into several pieces so it mixes easily into the dough.

Once the yeast is ready, pour the mixture into the bread machine canister (or mixer bowl). Add the flour, add the oil/butter.

If you can program your bread machine, set it for these three cycles: 15 minutes mix/knead; 20 minutes rest; 10 minutes mix/knead. If you aren't able to program your machine, simply use a timer to work through the cycles. If you're using a mixer, be sure to keep the dough covered and warm during the rest period. For each cycle, keep the mixer bowl and dough hook warm so it doesn't hamper your yeast action.

After the first five minutes of the initial mix/knead cycle, check the dough. If it's too sticky, add flour (2 tablespoons to ¼ cup at a time) until the dough is moist but doesn't stick to your hand. This dough tends to be somewhat drier than a white bread dough.

Once these three cycles are complete, prepare your bread pan by using non-stick spray, butter, oil, etc. You can shape the dough into a basic oblong roll. This dough will feel heavy and perhaps more dry than a white-bread dough. Cover the pan, place it in a warm location (i.e. the oven or stove top) and allow the dough to rise for 30 to 40 minutes, until the dough reaches at or slightly above the top of the pan. Multi-grain bread dough may sometimes require a longer rising period than white bread.

Once the dough has risen, preheat the oven to 350 degrees and bake for 30-40 minutes. Cool on a rack and refrigerate once it's cooled.

CLEAN EATING EZEKIEL BREAD HOMEMADE

6 Whole Grains
Healthy! Delicious!

CORNMEAL BREAD

This bread will pair beautifully with a hearty vegetable soup or taste divine with a butter and honey topping. Unlike cornbread, this loaf is light and airy with a slight cornmeal tang. I recommend using a fine ground cornmeal. You'll see the cornmeal bits in the crispy crust but there's no crunch in the bread itself. This recipe makes one large loaf (9x5 pan) or one medium loaf (8.5x4.5 pan) and two mini loaves. The mini loaves freeze well, giving you a delicious bread option in a short time.

1 cup water
1/3 cup milk
1/3 cup sugar, honey or maple syrup
3 teaspoons active dry yeast

1 egg at room temperature

3 to 4 cups all-purpose flour
1 ¼ cups cornmeal
1 ½ teaspoons salt
3 tablespoons butter/oil

Combine and warm the recipe liquids to a temperature range between 105 and 110 degrees.

Use a digital thermometer to verify the temperature. Dissolve the sweetener and measure the liquid temperature again. If it's less than 105, warm 2 or 3 tablespoons of the liquid and add back to the mixture until the desired temperature is reached. If it's too warm, allow it to cool. Dissolve the yeast and set aside while the yeast activates.

Measure and blend the flour, cornmeal, and salt. If using butter, cut it into small pieces.

Once the yeast is activated, place it in the bread machine canister. Add the flour mixture and the butter/oil.

BAKER'S TIP
When added to a bread dough recipe, both milk and egg enhance the soft texture and high rise of the dough.

If you can program your bread machine, set it for these three cycles: 15 minutes mix/knead; 20 minutes rest; 10 minutes mix/knead. If you aren't able to program your machine, simply use a timer to work through the cycles. If you're using a mixer instead of a bread machine, be sure to keep the dough covered and warm during the rest period. For each cycle, keep the mixer bowl and dough hook warm so it doesn't hamper your yeast action.

After the first five minutes of the initial mix/knead cycle, check the dough. If it sticks to your hand, add flour (2 tablespoons to ¼ cup at a time) until the dough is moist but doesn't stick to your hand.

Once the dough cycles are completed, place the dough in your pan(s). Cover and place in a warm location for the final rise. Once the dough is at or slightly above the top of the pan, preheat the oven to 350 degrees and bake for 30 minutes.

Once it's baked, immediately remove the bread from the pan and allow it to cool on a cooling rack. To store, place it in a plastic bag or bread keeper in the refrigerator.

NO-KNEAD ARTISAN BREAD

Want to mix up some dough, go to work, and come home and bake fresh bread for supper? Then you'll appreciate this overnight bread recipe.

This is a chewy bread with a crunchy crust, very much a contrast to a fine-crumb bread. For best results, use artisan bread flour, which has a higher percentage of protein than all-purpose flour. If you don't have artisan flour, you can add 3 tablespoons of wheat gluten (which is pure wheat protein) to the recipe.

To bake the bread, use a Dutch oven. If you don't have a Dutch oven, an oven-proof skillet or an oven-proof soup pot with a lid will work. If you want your bread to brown, replace ¼ to ½ cup of the artisan flour with whole wheat flour.

1 ½ cups water
3 cups artisan flour (or all-purpose + 1 tablespoon gluten)
2 tablespoons sugar, honey, or maple syrup
2 teaspoons salt
½ teaspoon active dry yeast

Warm the water to a temperature range between 105 and 110. Use a digital thermometer to verify the temperature. Dissolve the sugar and yeast in the water and allow the mixture to sit while you measure and blend the flour and salt. In a large bowl, slowly mix the yeast mixture into the flour. You will have a shaggy dough. Cover the bowl with plastic wrap and allow to sit at room temperature for 10 hours. In winter months, if the house is cool, you can warm your oven slightly (i.e. 100 degrees), then turn the oven off and let the bread proof in it.

As you prepare the bake the dough, place your Dutch oven/ pan in the oven and preheat the oven to 450 degrees. Allow 30 minutes for the Dutch oven to heat.

While the Dutch oven is heating, work the dough on a well-floured surface or parchment paper. This involves pulling and folding the dough to activate the gluten in your flour. With floured hands, form the dough into a ball. Loosely cover the dough with

plastic wrap and allow it to rest for 30 minutes.

Once the Dutch oven has heated, remove the lid. If you have a baker's peel, slide the dough into the Dutch oven and replace the lid. If you don't have a peel, be careful not to burn yourself as you place the dough into the Dutch oven and replace the lid. Bake the dough at 450 for 30 minutes. To finish the bread, remove the Dutch oven lid and bake for an additional 12 minutes.

Remove the bread from the Dutch oven and allow it to cool on a wired rack. And no, you don't have to wait till it's cooled before you enjoy a slice – or two!

BREAD MIXES

Bread mixes can be so handy when you're in a hurry, which seems like a daily condition in my household!

But commercial mixes aren't always easy to find, some are plenty expensive, and some don't offer much in the way of nutrition or flavor. So, here's how to make your own!

Creating your own bread mix will take some time. However, you'll be able to schedule this

> **BAKER'S TIP**
> Always label and date your flours to avoid using the wrong ingredient or making bread that ends up with poor flavor.

activity at a time when it's most convenient. If you organize it a bit like an assembly line, you'll be pleasantly surprised at how quickly you can make bread mixes that suit your personal bread baking goals and put less strain on both your grocery budget and your schedule.

Commercial bread mixes are likely to have some things your home-made mixes don't: artificial color, preservatives and highly processed flour(s). However, you aren't going to miss any of these ingredients when you prepare your own mixes.

To begin, select the bread recipe(s) you want to use. Make sure you have all the dry recipe

ingredients on hand to complete your mix. You won't be adding yeast, the recipe liquids, or butter/oil to these mixes.

For best results, aim to have flours, whole grains and/or other dry ingredients that are as fresh as possible. The fresher your ingredients, the better flavor you'll find in your bread. Processed flours – all-purpose and bread flour - have a shelf life of 12 months maximum. Storing flour, especially whole grain flour, in the freezer significantly extends its shelf life – to at least 12 or up to 18 months. You can store any type of flour in the freezer.

I've been successful using wide mouth quart jars or half-gallon jars to store my mixes, but plastic bags or other types of containers will work, too. You can use a funnel to help pour the recipe ingredients into a jar. If you're making several of the same mix, set up your jars like an assembly line, adding one ingredient at a time.

DON'T add the yeast to the flour mixture. Even commercial mixes come with a separate packet of yeast, so the yeast isn't affected by either the salt in the recipe or other recipe ingredients. When yeast comes in direct contact with salt, it dies.

If you want to, you can still measure the yeast and secure it in a small bag or container on top of the other ingredients. You might also wrap it up in plastic wrap. If your mix contains yeast, be sure it's stored in the refrigerator or freezer to retain the yeast quality.

No matter what type of container you use to store the mixes, I highly recommend labeling each one to record the type of bread (i.e., whole wheat, multi-grain, etc.) and the date you made the mix. This leaves no room for doubt about what the mix contains or its expiration date.

If you're creating multiple mixes, I've found that tucking the mixes into an oblong box that fits on my freezer shelf helps keep all the mixes together so I can easily see what I have on hand.

To cut down on time when you go to use your homemade mix, prepare all your utensils and remaining ingredients the night before or a few hours before you anticipate making the bread. This helps you complete the task quickly and efficiently.

SOURDOUGH BREAD

Sourdough bread continues to gain in popularity, and for good reason. Once you've mastered the process for making sourdough starter (see the steps in the front pages of this book) and using it to bake wonderful bread, you'll love baking this bread.

BAKER'S TIP
Sourdough breads are often slashed across the top of the loaf so strong yeast action doesn't blow out the side of the loaf.

For ideal results, feed your starter the night before you bake and allow your starter to set out at room temperature overnight.

There are multiple ways to use the "discard" that goes with feeding the starter. Of course, you can make pancakes or muffins. You can also make: crackers (numerous flavors), English muffins (they freeze well), tortilla chips, and more! My sourdough recipe is the result of numerous trials, researching, and reviewing

other recipes. You can mix this in the evening, allow it to sit on the counter overnight, place it in a pan, and bake it after a 3 to 6-hour rise time.

1/2 cup sourdough starter (at room temperature)
3/4 cup water
1/4 cup honey or sugar
3 - 4 cups all-purpose flour
1 1/2 teaspoons salt

Combine the flour and salt. Place the starter, honey, and water in the bread machine canister.

Blend the salt into the flour and add to the canister.

In the bread machine, repeat this cycle three times:
Mix 5 minutes - rest 5 minutes. Once those three cycles are complete, round the dough into a ball and place in a bowl coated with oil/vegetable oil. Cover the bowl and let it sit on the counter overnight.

After 10-12 hours, remove the cover, slip your fingers under the edge of the dough ball and pull it up into the center of the dough. Rotating the bowl, repeat this action, rotating around the bowl at least two times.

Shape the dough into a round ball and set it into a floured bowl or banneton or shape as an oblong roll and place in a traditional bread pan (not larger than 9x5). Allow the dough to raise for a minimum of three hours and up to six hours.

When the dough has raised satisfactorily, place it in the pan and preheat the oven to 350. Bake 35-40 minutes. Remove from the oven and slip the bread out of the pan. Allow it to cool on a rack. This bread will keep better at room temperatues than a loaf made with commercial yeast. However, if you don't plan to consume it within a couple of day, refrigeration is recommended.

SOURDOUGH BENEFITS

- Easy digestion
- Long shelf life
- Healthy for gut
- Inexpensive
- Just water and flour
- 0 preservatives
- Fresh from your oven
- Use for bread and baked goods
- Use for pancakes and waffles
- YUM!

GRANDMA'S SOURDOUGH

You don't have to make this bread at night, it's just convenient to have it rising while you sleep! You can use 100% white flour, white wheat flour, a mix of the two, or some whole wheat flour. At leasst 6 hours before stirring up your dough, feed your starter and leave it sit at room temperature to bring your starter to peak activity when you use it.

BAKER'S TIP
The key to making successful sourdough loaves lies partly in the kneading process, which helps develop the gluten fournd in flour and incorporates air, which gives the loaf a high rise.

ONE MEDIUM LOAF
1/2 cup sourdough (stirred down)
2-4 tablespoons honey
3/4 cup milk

3-4 cups flour
2½ teaspoons salt ≃ (

TWO MEDIUM LOAVES
1 cup sourdough (stirred down)

4 ½ - 5 1/2 cups organic all-purpose flour
4 teaspoons salt

¼ - 1/2 cup honey (1/2 cup for less tangy flavor)
1 2/3 cup water or milk

Place the sourdough starter in the bread machine canister (or mixing bowl). Add water and honey to sourdough. The more honey you use, the less prominent the sourdough flavor. Blend all the dry ingredients and add to the canister. Repeat this bread machine (or mixer) cycle 3 times: Mix/knead for 5 minutes. Rest for 5 minutes.

After the cycles complete, generously flour a bowl and your hands. Shape the dough into a ball, place in the bowl, cover the bowl and set in a warm place (i.e. an oven that's been warmed up to 100 degrees) for a minimum of 6 and up to 12 hours. A cooler temperature will result in a longer rise.

Your loaf is likely to be lighter with the longer rise, but a shorter rise also produces a satisfactory loaf.

After at least 6 hours, gently work the dough, slipping your fingers underneath the dough ball and pulling the outside to the middle. Rotating the bowl, repeat this motion for at least two rotations and up to three times.

When making two loaves, divide the dough in half (with a knife or bench scraper). Shape into either a dough ball to bake as a round loaf or oblong loaf to place in 8.5x4.5 or 9x5 coated bread pans. This dough works beautifully in a banneton. Cover the dough and set aside to raise for a minimum of three hours. When the dough has raised satisfactorily, preheat the oven to 400 degrees. If making a round loaf, carefully place it on a baking stone or in your preheated Dutch oven. Bake at 400 for 10 minutes, then 350 for 30 additional minutes. After removing from the oven, immediately place on a wire rack to cool.

Photos:
Left, at the beginning of the overnight rise. Right, ready to shape and place in a pan/banneton.

CINNAMON BREAD

You may notice that these recipe ingredients are the same as the cinnamon rolls. Depending on the size of loaf you desire, or the amount of cinnamon rolls you want, you can split this dough in half once it's ready to make both a small loaf of cinnamon bread and small batch of cinnamon rolls at the same time.

1 cup milk
1/3 cup sugar
3 teaspoons dry active yeast

BAKER'S TIP
Mini loaves of cinnamon bread are always a welcome gift!

2 eggs at room temperature

4 to 4 ½ cups flour all-purpose flour
1 ½ teaspoons salt
4 tablespoons butter
¼ cup sugar

Filling:
1/3 cup sugar
2 tablespoons cinnamon
1 tablespoon softened butter (to spread on dough)

Icing:
2 cups powdered sugar
1 teaspoon vanilla
3 to 6 tablespoons hot water

Warm the milk to a temperature range between 105 and 110 degrees. Use a digital thermometer to verify the temperature. Dissolve the sugar and measure the temperature again. If it's less than 105, warm 2 or 3 tablespoons of the liquid and add back to the mixture until the desired temperature is reached. If it's too warm, allow it to cool. Dissolve the yeast and set aside while the yeast activates.

Measure and blend the flour, salt and ¼ cup sugar. Cut the butter into small pieces.

Once the yeast is activated, place it in the bread machine canister. Add the flour mixture and the butter.

If you can program your bread machine, set it for these three cycles: 15 minutes mix/knead; 20 minutes rest; 10 minutes mix/knead. If you aren't able to program your machine, simply use a timer to work through the cycles. If you're using a mixer, be sure to keep the dough covered and warm during the rest period. For each cycle, keep the mixer bowl and dough hook warm so it doesn't hamper your yeast action.

After the first five minutes of the initial mix/knead cycle, check the dough. If it's too sticky, add flour (2 tablespoons to ¼ cup at a time) until the dough is moist but doesn't stick to your hand.

After the dough cycles are

completed, you can split the dough in half to make two one-pound loaves of cinnamon bread, or roll out in one oblong shape to make one loaf. After rolling out the dough, spread the butter across the length and width of it. Sprinkle the sugar/cinnamon mixture across the dough. Then roll up on the long side and pinch to seal. To obtain the optimum rise for small loaves, use bread pans that measure 4.5x8.5. A large loaf will require a 9x5 pan. Place the dough in your pan(s), cover the pan(s), allow the dough to rise in a warm location for 30-45 minutes.

Once the dough is at or slightly above the top edge of the pan,

heat the oven to 350 degrees and bake for 30 minutes and is nicely browned. Once it's baked, immediately remove the bread from the pan and cool on a rack. After it's cooled, store it in a bag or bread-keeper in the refrigerator.

For cinnamon rolls: see Cinnamon Roll recipe instructions.

CARAMEL ROLLS

Approximately 24 medium-size rolls

Many caramel roll recipes call for ingredients such as buttermilk or sour cream. I was delighted to come up with this simple but truly tasty recipe which uses just basic ingredients. If you don't have a bread machine, you can still make the recipe; just be sure to warm your milk to the appropriate temperature range and thoroughly knead your dough to help achieve a satisfactory rise. It's likely to quickly become your go-to recipe for sweet rolls!

1 cup milk
1/3 cup sugar
4 ½ teaspoons active dry yeast

3 1/3 – 4 cups flour
1/3 cup sugar
1 teaspoon salt
¼ cup butter, softened or chopped
1 egg, at room temperature, lightly beaten

Warm the milk to a temperature range of 105 to 110 degrees. Use a digital thermometer to verify the temperature. Dissolve the sugar in the milk and check the temperature again. If it's elow 105, warm it slightly on the stove top. Once the water is within the temperature range, dissolve the yeast in it and allow it to sit until the yeast is activated and bubbly.

While the yeast is activating, measure and mix the flour, sugar, and salt. Cut the ¼ cup butter into small pieces.

Once the yeast is ready, pour the mixture into the bread machine canister (or mixer bowl). Add the flour mixture and the butter.

If you can program your bread machine, set it for these three cycles: 15 minutes mix/knead;

20 minutes rest; 10 minutes mix/knead. If you aren't able to program your machine, simply use a timer to work through the cycles. If you're using a mixer, the cycle times are exactly the same. Be sure to keep the dough covered and warm during the rest period. For each cycle, keep the mixer bowl and dough hook warm so it doesn't hamper your yeast action.

After the first five minutes of the initial mix/knead cycle, check the dough. If it sticks to your hand, add flour (2 tablespoons to ¼ cup at a time) until the dough is moist but no longer sticks to your hand.

While the dough is in the bread machine, prepare the caramel topping and place it in a 9x13 cake pan. There's no need to coat the pan. The caramel will easily slip out.

Once the three bread machine cycles are complete, divide the dough into two pieces. Roll out one piece at a time on a silicone mat or well-floured surface. Spread one tablespoon of softened butter across the dough, then sprinkle the cinnamon/sugar mixture across the dough. From the long side, roll the dough up into a rope-shape. Cut into 10 or 12 pieces, placing each piece on top of the caramel topping.

Once the rolls are in the pan, cover them and allow them to rise in a warm location for 30 minutes. After 30 minutes, heat your oven to 350 degrees. Bake at 350-degrees for 25 minutes. If you wish, you can bake them for 30 minutes; just know the caramel may harden with the extended baking time.

Remove from the oven and immediately invert onto a plate or tray, taking care not to come in contact with the hot caramel.

These rolls are delicious hot or cooled. Enjoy!

Caramel topping
1 cup brown sugar, packed
1/3 cup butter
¼ cup corn syrup

Melt the butter; stir in the brown sugar and bring the mixture to a boil. Remove from heat and add the corn syrup, stirring to blend it in. While it's still hot, pour it into the 9x13-inch pan.

Filling
¼ cup brown sugar, packed
1 teaspoon ground cinnamon
2 Tablespoons softened butter

Using a small bowl, mix all ingredients and set aside.

CINNAMON ROLLS

Approximately 24 medium-size rolls

With or without icing, these traditional rolls are delightful right out of the oven!

1 cup milk
1/3 cup sugar
3 teaspoons dry active yeast

2 eggs at room temperature

4 to 4 ½ cups flour all-purpose flour
1 ½ teaspoons salt
4 tablespoons butter
¼ cup sugar

Filling:
1/3 cup sugar
2 tablespoons cinnamon
1 tablespoon softened butter (to spread on dough)

Icing:
2 cups powdered sugar
1 teaspoon vanilla
3 to 6 tablespoons hot water

Warm the milk to a temperature range between 105 and 110 degrees. Use a digital thermometer to verify the temperature. Dissolve the sugar and measure the temperature again. If it's less than 105, warm it slightly on the stove top until the desired temperature is reached. If it's too warm, allow it to cool.

Dissolve the yeast and set aside while the yeast activates.

Measure and blend the flour, salt and ¼ cup sugar. Cut the butter into small pieces.

Once the yeast is activated place it in the bread machine canister. Add flour mixture and the butter.

If you can program your bread machine, set it for these three cycles: 15 minutes mix/knead; 20 minutes rest; 10 minutes mix/knead. If you aren't able to program your machine, simply use a timer to work through the cycles. If you're using a mixer, be sure to keep the dough covered and warm during the rest period. For each cycle, keep the mixer bowl and dough hook warm so it doesn't hamper your yeast action.

After the first five minutes of the initial mix/knead cycle, check the dough. If it sticks to your hand, add flour (2 tablespoons to ¼ cup at a time) until the dough is moist but doesn't stick to your hand. After the dough cycles are completed, divide the dough into two pieces.

Roll each piece out to a rectangle. Use a butter knife, the back of a tablespoon, or a brush to spread the softened butter across the dough. Mix the cinnamon and 1/3 cup sugar and sprinkle across the dough as evenly as possible. From the long side, roll the dough tightly into a rope-like shape. Space the rolls evenly apart in a well-coated baking pan. Cover and allow them to raise for 30-45 minutes. Once they're raised, bake at 350 degrees for 25 minutes. Immediately remove from the pan and cool on a cooling rack.

To frost the rolls, place them on a tray or plate. Mix the powdered sugar, vanilla, and hot water. Spread over slightly cooled rolls. If there are rolls left, place them in a plastic bag, cover with plastic wrap, or place in a covered pan to prevent drying.

Approximately 18 medium-size rolls

STRAWBERRY DANISH

No need to be intimidated by the appearance of these delicious rolls. They are super easy to shape!

1 cup milk or half-and-half
1/3 cup sugar
4 teaspoons active dry yeast
3 – 4 cups flour
1/3 cup sugar
1 ½ teaspoons salt
¾ cup butter, softened/melted
3 egg yolks (at room temperature)

BAKER'S TIP
A pizza cutter works great for cutting bread dough for sweet rolls, breadsticks, etc.

1 cup strawberry jam or pie filling

Icing:
1 ½ cups confectioner's sugar
1 tablespoon butter, softened
¼ teaspoon vanilla
Dash of salt
2-3 tablespoons water/milk

Warm the milk to a range between 105 and 110 degrees. Use a digital thermometer to verify the temperature. Dissolve sugar in the milk. Use a digital thermometer to test the liquid's temperature. If it's less than 105, warm it on the stovetop. If it's too warm, allow it to cool. Once the temperature range is correct, dissolve the yeast and allow it to stand for approximately three minutes.

While the yeast activates, measure and blend the flour, sugar, and salt. Prepare the eggs and butter.

When the yeast has activated and the remaining dough ingredients are ready, place the yeast mixture into your bread machine (or mixer), add the flour, eggs, and butter.

Mix/knead the dough for 15 minutes. Place it in an oiled bowl, cover, and refrigerate overnight.

Since there's a lot of butter in this dough, it will be quite

stiff when you take it out of the refrigerator. You can warm your oven to about 100 degrees (then turn the oven off), and allow the dough to soften there for about 30 minutes.

Once the dough is ready to work with, divide it into two pieces. On a silicone mat or floured surface, roll each piece out in a four-inch-wide rectangle. Use a pizza cutter to cut one-inch strips all along the rectangle. Lay two strips side by side and twist them together in a rope-like shape. Pinch the ends together to form a circle. Keep in mind as you shape the rolls, they will double in size as they raise and bake.

Once you have shaped all the rolls, place them on a parchment-lined cookie sheet or cake pan.

Allow two inches between each roll so that, when they bake, they don't crowd together. This would keep the rolls from thoroughly baking. Cover the pan(s) and allow the rolls to rise in a warm location for 30 minutes.

When they're ready to bake use the end of a wooden spoon handle to create a ½-inch deep indentation in each roll. Spoon 1 tablespoon of jam or pie filling into each roll. Bake at 350 for 18-20 minutes, or until the rolls begin to brown. Remove from the oven and cool on a rack. Ice the rolls while they are slightly warm. These will freeze well if they aren't frosted.

SWEDISH TEA RING

Approximately 24 medium-size servings

I've been making this tea ring for years, but using the bread machine in the process makes it oh so easy!

1 cup milk
1 tablespoon dry active yeast
¼ cup sugar

3 ½ - 4 cups flour (either all-purpose or bread flour)
1/3 cup granulated sugar
1 1/2 teaspoons salt
¼ c butter, softened or chopped
1 egg, beaten

Filling
¼ cup brown sugar, packed
2 teaspoons ground cinnamon
2 Tablespoons softened butter
Chopped walnuts (optional)

Warm milk to temperature between 105- and 110-degrees. Use a digital thermometer to verify the temperature. Mix in granulated sugar, stirring to dissolve. Use a digital thermometer to verify

temperature range is accurate. If it's too cold, warm a small amount to reach proper temperature range. If it's too warm, allow it to cool. Once the temperature range is correct, add yeast, stirring to dissolve. Set the mixture aside for at least 3 minutes.

Using a small bowl, mix all dry ingredients and set aside. Use a fork or small whisk to beat the egg.

Pour the yeast mixture into your bread machine canister. Add the beaten egg; slowly add the flour mixture. Place the butter on top of the flour. Set the bread

machine on a cycle that includes: mix/knead (10-18 minutes) – 20-minute rest – mix/knead (10-18 minutes).

At any point during the mix/knead process you can prepare the filling.

Once the bread machine cycles are complete, use a sheet of parchment paper to roll the dough out into a rectangle shape. (This allows you to move the ring of dough to the baking sheet without distorting its shape.) Using a spoon or knife, spread the softened butter across the dough surface. Sprinkle the filling mixture evenly across the dough. Roll the rectangle into a tight rope-like shape. Seal edges with your fingers. You can stretch the dough slightly to even it out. Bring the two ends of the dough together and seal them together to create a ring. At 2-3 inch intervals, slash the top of the dough with a sharp knife.

Using the parchment paper, lift and transfer the dough to the baking sheet, retaining the parchment paper beneath it. Preheat the oven to 350 degrees and bake for 30-40 minutes or until the top of the ring is golden brown.

Again, using the parchment to move the ring, slide the ring onto a large plate, round platter, or round tray. Allow it to cool slightly before glazing with the frosting. To store any remaining pastry, cover and store in a cool place. It will keep for about 48 hours at room temperature or up to one week in the refrigerator.

BAKING NOTES

BAKING NOTES

CPSIA information can be obtained
at www.ICGtesting.com
Printed in the USA
LVHW072019180322
713830LV00003B/4